"Wisdom, courage, and inspiration are offered from this refreshing look at women in the Bible as each comes alive to recount her narrative as well as from the episodes Templeton reveals from her own life." Mary Jane Gorman, author of *Tending Body, Heart, Mind, & Soul: Following Jesus in Caring for Ourselves*

"'She couldn't possibly get that conclusion out of this scriptural account!' When I reread the scriptural account, in many cases, Templeton's interpretation was not only possible, but it opened new ways of thinking about the situation and the lessons to be learned." Reid Lehman, author of *God Wears His Own Watch*.

"Beth Lindsay Templeton invites us to sit on the porch with her and converse with women from the Bible who speak their stories of faith so we might listen anew in our own worlds." The Rev. Mary Abrams Morrison, Associate Executive for Vocations and Education, Foothills Presbytery, PC (USA); Past President, Association of Presbyterian Church Educators

Conversations on the Porch

To Sy' —
Blessings,
Beth Lindsay Templeton

Other Books by Beth Lindsay Templeton

Loving Our Neighbor: A Thoughtful Approach to Helping People in Poverty

Understanding Poverty in the Classroom: Changing Perceptions for Student Success

Conversations on the Porch

Ancient Voices—Contemporary Wisdom

Beth Lindsay Templeton

iUniverse, Inc.
Bloomington

Conversations on the Porch
Ancient Voices—Contemporary Wisdom

iUniverse books may be ordered through booksellers or by contacting:

iUniverse
1663 Liberty Drive
Bloomington, IN 47403
www.iuniverse.com
1-800-Authors (1-800-288-4677)

ISBN: 978-1-4620-5473-2 (sc)
ISBN: 978-1-4620-5475-6 (hc)
ISBN: 978-1-4620-5474-9 (e)

Printed in the United States of America

iUniverse rev. date: 11/14/2011

For Kathy, Jo, and Carol

Porch women

Contents

Part One: Women from the Old Testament

Acknowledgments

I thank the following people who helped prepare the ground for this book:

My mom, Dorcas Lindsay, who planted the seeds of yearning to write early in my life.

Dr. Doris Blanton, my creative writing teacher in high school, who taught me the basics of writing; Maria McKinney, who helped edit some of my early writings at United Ministries; and Lynne Shackelford, who encouraged my writing in numerous ways.

Penny Sisto, internationally known fabric artist, whose quilts opened the women's voices to me.

Will Thompson, clergy coach, who challenged me to hear what truths one woman in the Bible had for me. Listening to one led to listening to many.

The women of Circle #4 at Fourth Presbyterian Church in Greenville, SC, who continue to allow me to try new things and who encourage thoughtful wrestling with spiritual matters. They nurture my creativity when dealing with Biblical texts.

Carolyn Mathis and Elaine Nocks, who befriended me during the initial writing and who encouraged me to follow wherever the Spirit was leading me.

My husband, Jim Banks, who is my greatest cheerleader, my confidante, and my best friend.

Introduction

The screen porch addition to my house was my gift to myself. All the furniture is shabby. The cushions in the rocking chairs are flat in places. The current green color of the chairs is not original—obviously. Begonias, hostas, and ivy are exuberant in their variety of pots. Wind chimes sing as the breeze tickles the pipes. The three-story magnolia tree just beyond the steps embraces the porch with its wide, old branches. Dinner-plate-size white flowers release their lemony fragrance for all to enjoy.

I created the porch as a sanctuary for me. I realized that I might not always be able to leave town for a getaway, but I could always go to the porch and rock. Friends joined me and commented about what a special place it was for them as well. Some admitted that it was the only place in the world where they could truly relax. The porch became, for many who visited, a sacred place that nurtured their spirits. They found, if not answers, at least signposts for their journeys in life.

It was on this porch that conversations with women from the Bible took place. One summer afternoon, Eve appeared in the other rocking chair. Somehow, although I cannot tell you how, I knew she would share her life and be a guide for my journey.

After Eve's visit, others came. Occasionally several women would come in a week. At other times, days or weeks would pass before another guest arrived. The women did not appear in the order that their conversations are recorded in this book. The order of *Conversations on the Porch* grew out of the chronology of the Old and New Testaments.

Sometimes I would go to the porch having been overwhelmed by the day. Once I was thinking about a friend who was having trouble finding a position that used all her skills and talents. As I was rocking, grieving for my friend, I realized that Leah was sitting with me, watching the sun set over the roofs of the nearby homes. Another time, I was questioning my own inner wisdom because people around me were challenging my decisions and giving me reasons why I should do things differently. Lydia appeared and soothed my wounded spirit with her story. Over and over again, the women came to me, sharing their lives, offering their insights, and challenging me with new visions for how to live, what to care about, and how to use my passion and energy.

The women came from their places of power or powerlessness, with their strengths and vulnerabilities, and their successes and failures. They came to the porch to share their insights and guidance. These sacred visitors embraced me with their wisdom, their love, and their passion. They rocked in the chairs and asked that whoever would listen, should listen. They are depending on us to hear their ancient voices as we move into our own renewed and expanded visions of life as people of God. They challenge us to embrace living as they did and to continue the conversations.

I've been asked if the women appeared "bodily as with flesh and blood." That's a difficult question. To me, each woman was real. Whether she was visible to the eye or only to my heart and mind is inconsequential to the wisdom she shared. You can determine for yourself the answer to this question.

How to Use This Book

A reminder of the call(s) to action that the guest issued during her visit immediately follows each conversation. Please consider her comments in light of your own experiences and expectations. If you are reading *Conversations on the Porch* by yourself, you may want to record your thoughts and feelings in a journal. If you are using this book in a group, you can use the questions for discussion.

"Porch Breezes" offers tidbits to ponder that were brought in by the spirit-wind. The breezes include Scripture verses, quotes, and occasionally, resources. Just as a summer breeze entices you at times to revel in its coolness and at other times blows by without notice, so these brief sayings will either inspire you to further contemplation, or they will simply float by without requiring any consideration.

It is my hope that you will find the conversations with these holy women as soothing and motivating as I did.

Blessings,

Beth Lindsay Templeton

Part One 🌿

Women from the Old Testament

Chapter One
Eve—Blame and Grief

Genesis 2:4–4:26

Eve was the first woman in history, wife of Adam and mother of Cain, Abel, and Seth. She ate the fruit of the Tree of Knowledge of Good and Evil at the urging of the serpent. She gave some of the beautiful fruit to Adam, and they both saw things they had not noticed before, such as the fact that they had no clothes. The Lord God was displeased. Adam and Eve were exiled from their homeplace.

The need to rock on the porch that afternoon was painfully strong. A friend's grandchild had just been diagnosed with cancer. She was devastated by the potential loss of a beloved three-year-old granddaughter. Her grief was raw in those early days of the diagnosis. I went to the porch to soothe my own feelings of helplessness as I thought about her fear. While I was rocking, I remembered a time when my own family lost a child to death.

It shouldn't have happened. My brother should not have been born dead. If the doctor … if the nursing staff … if my mother … if, if, if. My brother should have been healthy. He was fully formed and beautiful. My mother blamed herself. The open windows in the houses on both sides of ours allowed the torturous sounds of babies' crying in the night to come into my mother's bedroom. She was extremely depressed for a year.

My brother's death happened when I was six years old. At that time, life as I had known it was over. Death had entered my family and taken away my carefree mother. Now, as an adult, I tried to imagine what my mother's feelings had been when she realized that her precious son would never reach out to her for sustenance. I remembered my own miscarriage; the pain of women who lived in poverty and whose children were condemned to inadequate medical care; and the grief of women who experienced a child's unexpected or untimely death. Even though I tried to connect in my heart with my mother's pain, I knew that I barely touched her feelings of grief.

As our family learned to deal with the tragedy of our loss, I became increasingly responsible around the house. When my last brother was born two years later, I was called "little mother" because I was so involved in his daily care. I enjoyed the responsibility most of the time. However, as I rocked now on my porch, I remembered a perceived wrong when I was held responsible for something my brothers had done. I had to admit I had spent a lot of personal energy in other instances in my life declaring that I was innocent. If he had only … When you … I did not …

As I tried to wrap my thoughts and feelings around this collage of memory being stirred up, I realized that I was no longer alone. I had not heard anyone come onto the porch. I thought the screen door was locked. As I looked more closely, I was shocked. The person sat down in the rocking chair beside me even though I knew I had never met this uninvited "guest." I had no idea who this … woman? … was or how she'd gotten there.

I decided that the best course of action was to pretend that no one else was on the porch with me. Maybe then I'd realize I was dreaming and that I was not, really, I was not crazy!

I closed my eyes. After a minute or two of hearing only the birds in the tree, I peeked with one eye open. She was still there!

Since Plan A of pretending nothing had happened did not work, I went for Plan B and the confrontational approach. "Who are you and what are you doing here?"

She replied in a melodic, yet throaty voice, "My name is Eve."

"What's your last name?"

"I am Eve, wife of Adam. You know, in the Bible?"

"Oh," I squeaked, as if biblical women appeared on my porch every day. I rocked and rocked, back and forth. Neither of us spoke. I tried very hard to listen to my internal sense of guidance, and still I rocked. My experience with spiritual imagination had sometimes taken me to very provocative places in my understanding of holy connections. I decided to allow my imagination to explore with this woman who called herself "Eve."

So I said, "Hello. May I call you Eve? Mother Eve?"

"Mother Eve sounds nice."

"Oh, okay, Mother Eve. What do we do now?"

"Dear child, I wonder if you have any questions you'd like to ask me."

"Huh? Well, since you're here, I do have a question for you. I know that you have wisdom born from eating fruit from that tree in the garden of Eden as well as from your life journey. What can you teach me from your experiences for my own life? What path would you call me to walk?"

To my astonishment, this is what she said:

"My child, thank you for seeking my insights. Many damn me for my part in displeasing God. Some people wish that I never existed. Women curse me because of the pain they suffer in childbirth. Men curse me because they must labor hard to earn a living. People of faith blame me for bringing sin into the world. With so many people shunning me, I am delighted that you believe I have something to offer.

"In the beginning, God created Adam and me, so I'll start there. In one of our conversations as we were exploring our relationship with each other, Adam mentioned to me that he had chatted with God about the animals. He delighted me with tales of deciding names for all of them. Don't you think *penguin* and *aardvark* are funny? He told me about a tree in the garden that had fruit he could not eat because he would die. I trusted that my husband had indeed conversed with this God, but I, to that point, had never had any direct contact with the Creator.

"Adam and I spent a lot of time together, obviously, since there was no one else around. When he was not in a talkative mood, I was left with no one to share my thoughts and dreams. That infamous day when the serpent showed up and began talking with me was thrilling. Not only did I have someone to talk with, but the conversation about God and the root of knowledge was stimulating and thought-provoking. How was I supposed to know that the snake did not have my best interests at heart? After all, my experience in these things was rather limited, to say the least.

"The serpent was engaging and made the fruit appear tantalizing, so I ate. I offered some to Adam that he willingly ate. When God found out what we had done, Adam blamed the Creator for giving me to him, and Adam also blamed me for giving him the fruit. I, I'm not proud to admit, blamed the snake for our folly.

"I urge you to learn from my mistake. Take full responsibility for your decisions and actions. It is true the serpent encouraged me to do something I knew I should not do—eat forbidden fruit. However, I felt justified making the decision even when it turned out badly. I now know that I had a choice. I had an option. The snake did not pick up the fruit and put it to my mouth, make me bite it and eat it. The snake did not give the fruit to Adam and force him to eat. I—I picked the fruit. I put its beautiful shape, color, and taste to my lips. I savored it. I enticed Adam to share this delicious nectar. He willingly bit into the fruit's flesh. Adam and I ate of our own choice. God did not make us do it. The serpent did not make us do it.

"Accepting responsibility is not an easy thing to do. It seemed far easier to us to try to hide. We should have known that we could not hide for very long from God, for heaven's sake. We could not even hide from ourselves. Let me save you some time and grief. Just accept responsibility and do not spend your energy denying and avoiding your decision or action.

"Things went downhill from there. Don't get me wrong. We did not fear that we had been cast from the love of God. God could have just killed us right then and started all over with a better, more perfect design. For some unknown, convoluted, yet holy reason, God kept working with us. I know that we tried God's patience.

"God explained to us that from now on, our tasks on the earth would be hard. For me, as a woman, childbirth would not be easy. Was that an understatement! And Adam would have to work in the heat, cold, drought, and flood to put food on the table. Neither of us had a magic potion that we could use to get what we wanted. We were growing painfully in maturity.

"We did not appreciate what we had had before our betrayal of God, because the garden with all its bounty had simply been handed to us. Now we appreciated everything—our three children, our food, our clothing, and our home. Make sure that you appreciate your blessings. Offer thanks for the people and things in your life, no matter how insignificant they may be. I never thought that a handful of moss soaked in cool water could feel so good until I was drenched with the sweat of birth labor. Adam thanked God daily for earthworms that helped him break up the packed soil of his fields.

"Now, child, I need to share with you something that a mother hopes she will never have to face. One of my sons, Cain, killed another of my sons, Abel. I ask that you walk with people who suffer that grief. Losing a child, for whatever reason—sickness, murder, war, starvation—is too horrible to grasp. I would not ask you to imagine what I went through. However, I can ask you to be aware of the pain that parents face when losing a child. Not only did I lose Abel, but also I lost Cain, because he was banished from our family. He was, thank God, under God's protection, even with all he had done. Cain married and had children, but I could not be blessed by having those dear grandchildren with me as I grew old. Therefore, the agony of my loss continued even after the devastating grief following Abel's death subsided."

At this point Mother Eve stopped talking, rocked rapidly, and wiped tears that slipped down her wrinkled cheeks.

"Sorry. I lost my train of thought as I remembered my yearning for my family. Where was I? Oh, right. When parents lose a child, they never totally close the hole in their hearts. Be present for those grieving parents.

"But since I am the mother of all humanity, I charge you to care for all the children of all the mothers of the earth. Every person who dies or is killed by human cruelty or neglect or ignorance is also my child. Please stop the killing and dying of children.

"Do you know the pain of a mother when one child dies? Do you know how it feels to have a child sent away from you to war, exile, death, or debilitating illness? How can you not feel the pain of all the mothers and grandmothers? How can you not see what is happening to all the children of the world?

"I apologize. I know that you are only one person, and you are not responsible for all the pain and torment in the world. I get carried away when I remember my losses. But you are *one* person and you can do *something*.

"Show me how you love me, Eve, your mother, by working to stop the killing, in whatever form it takes. Prevent anyone else from going through what I did. Please, I pray you, my daughter."

When Eve finished, I could only sit in silence and amazement. Then she said, "More women whom you know from your studies and reading of the Holy Bible will come. They are guides to share with you what they know from their experiences. Ask them for their wisdom and insights. Their ancient voices have current value, as you will soon discover."

And then I was alone, as if what had just happened had never happened. But my heart was full, my head was clear, and my spirit was soothed. If I was crazy because I was thinking that the past few moments had been truly, actually real, then I loved it! I'd just be crazy!

Eve's Call to Action

- Take full responsibility for your decisions and actions.

- Make sure that you appreciate your blessings. Offer thanks for the people and things in your life, no matter how insignificant they may be.

- Walk with people who suffer the grief of losing a child.

- Care for all the children of all the mothers of the earth. Please stop the killing and dying of children.

- Show me how you love me, Eve, your mother, by working to stop the killing, in whatever form it takes. Prevent anyone else from going through what I did.

Your Response to Eve's Presence

1. Do any of Eve's calls challenge you in your own life or community? If so, how?

2. Does her journey stir up a story for you? If so, what?

3. What did you learn from listening to Eve?

4. Does her story inspire you to action? If so, what? When? How? Why?

Porch Breezes

Somewhere in the world, a child dies of hunger every five seconds. That is six million children a year, 16,000 a day.[1]

The Annie E. Casey Foundation has a database about the well-being of children that is organized by state and region. You can look up Kids Count on your search engine to find out what is going on in your area.[2]

"To find fault is easy; to do better may be difficult."[3]

Chapter Two

Sarah—Promises and Joy

Genesis 12:1–13:1; 16:1–16; 17:15–16; 18:1–15; 21:1–14

Sarah was the wife of Abraham and the mother of Isaac.

I worked with a life coach for several months and found the experience, for the most part, to be wonderful and helpful. I began to identify some of the issues that were important for the next steps of my career path. I also claimed some of the fears that were hindering me from taking those next steps. I valued working with someone who tapped into my skills and inner knowledge, who gently questioned me in caring ways, and who listened to me, without interruption, for as long as I needed, within the framework upon which we had agreed.

My coach saw strengths and gifts in me that I could not. He challenged me to let my free spirit come out to play, unleashing creative surges that felt invigorating. However, I began to feel that it was my responsibility to make the next steps of my future happen. I became anxious that maybe I was not doing enough, taking enough risks, or pushing myself hard enough in order to live into my future. Not only did pursuing goals aggressively not feel comfortable to me, but forcing open the doors to my future did not correspond with my understanding of how God worked with me.

Yet I knew there was more for me. I knew that God was leading me to something else. How, where, and when were the big unknowns. As I sat on the porch and tried to relax into my God-given future, whenever, whatever, and wherever it might be, I smelled the refreshing fragrance of the magnolia blossoms. I watched a housefly beat against the porch screening in its efforts to be free. I heard a lawn mower down the street. I rocked, I smelled, I watched, and I heard. Then I noticed that once again someone was sitting with me. She was very old but stately in her demeanor. I was not as shocked this time but was unsure of the protocol for greeting the women who appeared on my porch.

"Hello," I said.

"Greetings," she said.

"May I ask your name?"

"Certainly. I am known now as Sarah."

"Sarah, wife of Abraham and mother of Isaac?"

"The one and the same."

I rocked more quickly as I absorbed this information. Then I realized I wanted to ask Sarah for her wisdom and counsel as Mother Eve had suggested. I slowed my back and forth motion to almost no movement and said, "You journeyed far both in faith and in travel with your husband, Abraham. From your vantage point as Abraham's wife, what do you offer me? What can I learn from your legacy and how can I honor you?"

"My child, indeed I have journeyed far. As a young bride in Haran, my husband, known as Abram at the time, decided that his God was calling him, and therefore me, to leave everything we knew and go to the land that God was giving to us. When Abram announced this to me, I could not believe what he was saying. He was abandoning his family and his responsibilities in Haran; he was asking me to leave the comfortable life that I had always known; and he was expecting me to join him willingly and with a sense of excitement. He told me that his God had promised to make him a great nation and would bless him. His God had not told these things to *me*. I wondered if Abram was simply making this up or if he truly had had a direct encounter with the Holy One.

"It really did not matter if I believed Abram or not. We were leaving. Lot, his nephew, chose to accompany us on this adventure with its rich promises. We became wanderers, claiming the land that God told Abram was his. We stopped and built an altar in Shechem. From there we moved on to the hill country east of Bethel and built another altar. By stages we moved to the Negeb. I held on to the promise that Abram said God had made—that Abram would be a great nation and would be blessed. I kept waiting to become pregnant so that my husband could begin welcoming his heirs for this great nation. But it did not happen.

"Actually, neither of us felt very blessed. The land that supposedly was ours to claim was not rich and fertile. The more we traveled, the more sand I seemed to eat and the less food we were able to gather. Because of the famine, Abram announced that we were traveling to Egypt, where he would get herds and slaves. Always the dreamer, my husband!

"Once again he astounded me. As we were getting close to Egypt, Abram said to me, 'Sarai, you are so beautiful. I love you dearly. I need you to help me with one small thing.'

"It had been so long since he had noticed me as a woman that I was thrilled. I breathlessly told him I would gladly do whatever he asked of me. Little did I know what was coming next. He wanted me to pretend to be his sister. He knew that if it were known that I was Abram's wife, Pharoah would kill *him* to get *me* as his own. since I was still beautiful. To protect his own life, Abram decided to deceive the ruler of Egypt.

"I thought the whole scheme was preposterous. I agreed to go along with it, assuming it would never happen. As it turned out, Abram was right. Pharoah did want to claim my beauty as his own. I never mentioned to him that I was Abram's wife. I lived with the lie. In return for my services with Pharoah, Abram received sheep, oxen, male and female donkeys, male and female slaves, and camels (as per Genesis 12:16). I *told* you I was beautiful! I was worth every one of those gifts … and more.

"When plagues began to come to his house, Pharoah began to suspect that everything was not as Abram had presented it. He realized that I was Abram's wife and not his sister.

"Pharoah confronted Abram. I knew both of us would be killed. However, I underestimated the esteem in which Pharoah held me. He granted that Abram and I, along with our household, could leave, taking all the magnificent gifts he had given to us. When we returned to the Negeb, we went back to where we had started, to the place between Bethel and Ai. We were now very rich.

"As we began to settle into the life God had promised us, Abram announced that the Lord God kept talking about his offspring. I still had not become pregnant. Abram had no children by other women. Now that I was getting older, I did not know how this promise was going to be fulfilled. I decided to take matters into my own hands. I offered Abram my servant, Hagar, as his concubine. Since I owned her, whatever children she had with Abram would be mine.

"I never considered how I would feel when I saw Hagar getting bigger and bigger with Abram's child. She became contemptuous of me. My life once again became miserable. First I had to leave my childhood home and wander through the desert. Then I became the wife of Pharoah even though I was already married to Abram. Then I was taunted by a mere slave because she had been able to give my husband what I could not. I confess that I was as mean to her as I felt she was to me. She ran away and I was glad. But then she returned. I swallowed my pride and allowed her to come into my tent again because she was the instrument of God's giving Abram the offspring he was promised.

"Abram came in from tending the flocks one evening and announced that from then on, he would be called Abraham. He said the Lord had promised to make him the ancestor of a multitude of nations and that kings would come from him. Then he said that my name was now Sarah, but he would not tell me why. He could not keep from laughing when he told me what he was going to call me. I thought he was an old fool, with him being one hundred and me ninety years old!

"Shortly after that, three men appeared at our encampment. As was the way of our people, we offered them water, bread, and refreshment. While they were waiting for the feast to be prepared, they made what I thought was small talk until I heard one of them say, 'I will surely return to you in due season, and your wife Sarah shall have a son' (Genesis 18:10). I could only laugh. I was too old! But he did know my name was now Sarah. Unfortunately, he heard me laughing. Even though I denied it, he said, 'Oh yes, you did laugh' (Genesis 18:15).

"Abraham's God finally convinced me that holy promises could happen without my help. To this point, I had tried to work out God's will for Abraham in the only way I could. I agreed to every one of his crazy schemes and even came up with the one about Hagar on my own. This time, however, there was absolutely nothing I could do. I had ceased in my monthly courses. There was no way that I could get pregnant.

"But God had the laugh this time. I did become pregnant with my son, Isaac. Being a first-time mother at my age was both a joy and, I have to admit, a challenge, but one I welcomed with all my heart.

"I could not fully enjoy my life, however, as long as Hagar and her son, Ishmael, were around. Every time I looked at Ishmael, who looked so much like his father, I lost some of my joy. When I acknowledged to myself that Ishmael was the firstborn, I got angry. *I* was the one who had been on the entire journey with Abraham. *I* was the one who suffered the indignities of Pharoah. *I* was the one who had been given a miracle baby. There was no way that *I* was going to let that woman and her child usurp the rightful place of my son. I told Abraham to send her away. And he did.

"When I wake up in my bed at night, I think back over my life. I remember how I tried to make God's plan work and did not trust the Lord God Almighty. I regret what I did to Hagar in giving her to my husband. I did not trust God to fulfill God's promises to you. I rejoice in my son and in the future into which he walked. For much of my life, I did not walk with faith in God. It took a blessed baby to convince me that our God is gracious and true to God's promises. I hope and pray that you will not have to be as old as I was before you can live joyfully in God's grace. May your faith guide you. May God's joy be your own."

I closed my eyes to absorb all that Sarah had told me. When I opened them, she was gone.

Sarah's Call to Action

+ Trust the Lord God Almighty and do not try on your own to make God's plan work.

+ Trust God to fulfill God's promises to you.

+ Live joyfully in God's grace.

Your Response to Sarah's Presence

1. Do any of Sarah's calls challenge you in your own life or community? If so, how?

2. Does Sarah's journey stir up a story for you? If so, what?

3. What did you learn from listening to Sarah?

4. Does Sarah's story inspire you to action? If so, what? When? How? Why?

Porch Breezes

"Blessed be the Lord, for he has heard the sound of my pleadings. The Lord is my strength and my shield; in him my heart trusts; so I am helped, and my heart exults, and with my song I give thanks to him" (Psalm 28:6–7).

"Can we take the time to learn more richly to love and enjoy the gifts of creation and of the neighbors around us? Can we let the saints of the Christian community teach us to rest deeply in the grace of the moment and the place, in the fullness of God's love throughout time and space?"[4]

"It has always been a mystery to me how men can feel themselves honored by the humiliation of their fellow-beings."[5]

Chapter Three

Hagar—Abuse, Forgiveness, and God's Presence

Genesis 16, 21:1–21

Hagar was Sarah's slave brought from Egypt. Sarah gave Hagar to Abraham so her husband could have a child. After she became pregnant, Hagar ran away and encountered God. She alone, of everyone in the Hebrew Scriptures, called God by name—El-roi—and remained alive. She returned to give birth to Abraham's son, Ishmael. After Sarah's son, Isaac, was born, Hagar was permanently banished. The Lord came to her again for protection. From her lineage comes the vast group of people who worship through the religion of Islam.

It had been a particularly trying day at work. A friend and former prostitute had been working in a fast-food restaurant for more than two years. While at work, she fell and significantly damaged her back. She informed me that day that the company refused to file a workers' compensation claim for her. She was in pain and I was angry. She had kicked her drug habit, left prostitution, repaired her bad credit, and she was holding a legitimate job. She was earning less than seven dollars an hour and had no benefits. She was doing what society expected of her, and she still was being put down and denied access to services that were rightfully hers. It was not a good day.

Almost as soon as I sat down in my rocking chair on the porch, I was joined by a woman who identified herself as Hagar. My eyes widened and my pulse quickened when I realized who was sitting with me.

I said, "Hello, Mistress Hagar. You saw the Lord. You bore both blessing and curse because of your relationship with Abraham, Sarah, and Ishmael. What path are you calling me to?"

She replied, "I fear you. People who have befriended me have shown me they are not my friends. I have been a pawn in other peoples' plans, which is not a comfortable place to be. I was used as a slave; I was used by Abraham so he could get an heir; I was used by Sarah so she could give her husband a child. Used—used—used.

"To them I was a nobody. Abram and Sarai did not even call me by my name! I was simply a way for them to get what they wanted. I was only property, a thing.

"Please, please don't use people as I was used. I wanted Sarai and Abram to recognize that I was not beneath them. I was still a person with hopes and dreams of my own. I had visions for my life that were bigger than being used by them, bigger than being their servant. I performed menial jobs in taking care of Sarai. I wanted her to appreciate my service to her. I needed her to acknowledge how I had helped her have the life of her choosing. I yearned for her to recognize my dignity. When she did not, well, then I regret to say, I developed an attitude toward her.

"Please, please do not use people as I was used.

"I cannot say that my life was totally bad. I gave life to my darling Ishmael. Even though his existence caused me to be cast away, I am proud of him and who he became. He married a lovely girl from Egypt!

"Because of my love of and for him, I remind you to look for God's blessing even when life demeans you and people mistreat you. If you cannot immediately see the good in your situation, keep looking.

"It took me a while to see how blessed my life had become when I was exiled from Sarai and Abram. I finally realized I was no longer a slave! I was on my own in the wilderness. That was scary and depressing at first. I thought my child and I were going to die from dehydration. I did not know where to turn.

"Then the Lord of Abram and Sarai came to me in the desert, called me by name (something neither of them ever did), comforted, and supported me. I was frightened. Then I was angry. Then I was encouraged. Then I had hope. I knew that Ishmael and I would survive. That was when I realized what a gift I had with my freedom and my son. So remember, bad situations can lead to good.

"My son, Ishmael, lost his birthright. As Abram's firstborn, he should have received his father's blessing. Sarai made sure that did not happen. I will not forgive her for that denial.

"On the other hand, when we were sent away, Ishmael no longer had to bow down to his father. He was no longer the son of a slave, since I was no longer in slavery! Ishmael was free to find his own way, which he did. He sired the people who worship Allah, the followers of Islam.

"At first I thought all was lost. But because the Lord of Sarai and Abram watched over Ishmael and me, we more than survived. We thrived!

"I leave you with two other lessons to consider. The first is one I do not like to admit. I *never* forgave Sarai. She had Isaac and was honored along with Abram. I, however, was a nobody who wandered in the wilderness after being exiled. Once she sent me away, Sarai forgot about me. I, unlike Sarai, was not remembered kindly in the history of the Christian church. As far as Sarai was concerned, I no longer existed. But she definitely existed for me. Every day, I fed my hatred of her. I drank deeply of my bitterness.

"Now I can see that my hatred of her did not affect her at all. I was affected. I became a bitter woman. I hope you will seek to forgive those who have wronged you—not for the other person's sake, but for your own. My life would have been more joyful and satisfying if I could just have forgiven her.

"My other lesson is to know that God is always with you. When my life looked the bleakest, God showed up in the most amazing ways. When other people intend to do you harm, God can help you see possibility and claim hope. God can come to you in ways most appropriate for you.

"I am a strong woman. God came to me in a strong and direct way when I was feeling most defeated. Trust that God can do the same for you in ways that are utterly right for you.

"I do not wish my path for you. Even so, I would not trade my journey. I encountered the Holy God in an amazing manner. I have Ishmael. I *thrived*! Ultimately, what more could I ask?"

"Thank you, Mistress Hagar. You have given me much to ponder." In no more than the blink of an eye, she had left me.

Hagar's Call to Action

- Please, please don't use people as I was used.

- Look for God's blessing even when life demeans you and people mistreat you. If you cannot immediately see the good in your situation, keep looking.

- Remember that bad situations can lead to good.

- Seek to forgive those who have wronged you—not for the other person's sake, but for your own.

- Know that God is always with you.

Your Response to Hagar's Presence

1. Do any of Hagar's calls challenge you in your own life or community? If so, how?

2. Does Hagar's journey stir up a story for you? If so, what?

3. What did you learn from listening to Hagar?

4. Does Hagar's story inspire you to action? If so, what? When? How? Why?

Porch Breezes

"You shall love your crooked neighbor with your crooked heart."[6]

"And remember, I am with you always, to the end of the age" (Matthew 28:20).

> And why do we struggle to forgive? Why do we decide we will do the work that forgiveness requires? Because God forgives us, because forgiveness is a matter of faith. We also

forgive because forgiveness gives us freedom—freedom from the pain and from being hurt easily. Forgiveness heals the forgiver. It may not affect the person who did the offense at all. The person may not even know that he or she did anything that warrants forgiveness. The other person does not have to do anything or change behavior or be a certain way for us to forgive. We may not even share with the people who hurt us that we have forgiven him or her or them. But when we forgive, our hearts will open and we will have an open heart.

And maybe that's the point of forgiving—so that we can love as God loves, so we can be present for everyone who comes in our path, and so we can hear the other person's pain without being consumed with our own. In forgiveness, we open our hearts to God and to our fellow journeyers.[7]

Chapter Four

Leah—Settling for Less and Caring for Others

Genesis 29–31

Leah was Jacob's first wife but not his first choice. She was the mother of Reuben, Simeon, Levi, Judah, Issachar, Zebulun, and Dinah, and the aunt to Joseph and Benjamin, her sister Rachel's sons.

~&

Women with seminary educations rarely become the senior pastor of a large congregation, even after years of serving as ordained ministers. They become chaplains, nonprofit managers, caseworkers, pastoral counselors, associate pastors for education, writers, pastors of small congregations, spiritual advisors, workshop leaders, or "freelance" ministers who preach when the "regular" pastor is sick, on vacation, or on sabbatical. Some work as interim ministers, helping congregations emotionally say good-bye to a beloved former pastor and hello to a new sense of ministry with a new minister.

Most clergywomen seem content with the life of ministry that they've been able to carve out for themselves. However, some still itch to be seen as a "real minister" (i.e., the pastor of a congregation that has enough members to have program staff and multiple worship services each week). These women are still ministers, but not in the way they imagined when God planted the dream of ordained ministry in their lives.

As I remembered a conversation with a woman who yearned to move from the small church she was pastoring to a larger flock, I noticed a breeze on my legs from the movement of the rocking chair beside me. I looked over and smiled a greeting.

Leah smiled back as she introduced herself.

"Hello. I'm glad to meet you, Leah. You have lived a life full of lessons. Will you please share some of them with me?"

She opened with, "I *have* lived quite a life, my child. Where do I begin? I guess I begin with that day when Jacob first came to our land. When he saw my younger sister, Rachel, as she worked the sheep, I think he fell in love immediately. Jacob talked with my father, Laban, about what Jacob had to do to claim Rachel as his wife. My father told Jacob that he had to work seven years for him, and then he could have Rachel.

"That plan both infuriated me and pleased me. I was angry that my little sister was promised when the pledge should have been made for me. I was the eldest and by rights should have married first. It's not that I'm ugly or anything. I have been told many times how beautiful my eyes are. The commitment should have been mine.

"I was also pleased. You see, I loved Jacob from the first time I saw him. I loved his manliness. I loved his ambition. I knew that he would be a bountiful provider. I secretly hoped that my father's seven-year delay in Jacob's claiming of my sister would allow me time to win his love. I think I even convinced myself that Jacob had developed a tender spot in his heart for me.

"When the seven years were completed, I realized that Rachel was still the woman whom Jacob desired. How can I describe my devastation? She was taking my love. *She* was going to be his wife. *She* was going to give him babies. And I? I would be shuffled aside, probably only to serve as caregiver to *her* children. I was ready to die. I certainly did not believe in Jacob's God. His God had stolen from me the only thing I ever wanted in life … Jacob!

"My father slipped into my quarters one afternoon when I was alone and shared with me his devious plan. He would substitute me for Rachel under the wedding canopy. The wedding veils would keep me covered until after Jacob had taken me physically as his own. Out of my weakness of disappointment and unreturned love, I agreed to my father's plot.

"Even then I hoped that Jacob would not be angry and would love me with his whole heart. How foolish I was. As soon as my husband realized what had happened, he raged at my father: 'What is this you have done to me? Did I not serve with you for Rachel? Why then have you deceived me?' (Genesis 29:25). I was humiliated and felt worthless.

"My father gave Rachel as wife to Jacob a week after our own wedding. My husband had to work another seven years as payment for Rachel.

"Before our fruitfulness was ended, Jacob had two wives, two maids, twelve sons, and one daughter. I am proud to claim that seven of those children came from my womb. Needless to say, this did not sit well with my sister, who was barren for many years while I regularly birthed children.

"My life was not unbearable. I had the respect of our household because of the multiple times I enlarged our family. I was married to Jacob, which was my wish.

"Along with getting my wish, however, I reaped a lifetime of sadness. I went through life knowing that my husband felt he had been betrayed and that I was part of that betrayal. I lost my close relationship with my sister because of Jacob's coming between us. I lost my father in my heart because of how I had been manipulated by him to be a pawn in his quest of greed. I was surrounded by people—children, maids, men who worked with my husband, and their families—and I never felt truly loved.

"I managed to convince myself that I was willing to settle for second best. I chose to allow myself to be satisfied with the leftovers of love rather than drinking from the overflow of a husband's heart. I substituted the love of and for my children for the love I craved from the man to whom I was bound for a lifetime.

"My call to you is to care for yourself when you feel you have lost. Reach out to other people who lose. Find ways to affirm others when they feel they are having to settle for less than they desire. Discover ways to affirm your dignity and self-worth—ways that are not dependent on another's affirmation of you. Walk as a companion with people who feel forgotten. Hold their hands and help them claim their God-given value that is unique to them. Help them appreciate the gifts they already have—whatever or whomever they may be.

"I know what second best feels like. Hold my hand and we'll walk the journey together. You'll see. There will be many good things that will happen along the way. Such is life!"

"Oh, Leah. Your words are wise. I will think deeply upon them. Thank you."

We rocked together for a while and then she was gone.

Leah's Call to Action

- Care for yourself when you feel you have lost.

- Reach out to other people who lose.

- Find ways to affirm others when they feel they are having to settle for less than they desire.

- Discover ways to affirm your dignity and self-worth—ways that are not dependent on another's affirmation of you.

- Walk as a companion with people who feel forgotten. Hold their hands and help them claim their God-given value that is unique to them. Help them appreciate the gifts they already have—whatever or whomever they may be.

Your Response to Leah's Presence

1. Do any of Leah's calls challenge you in your own life or community? If so, how?

2. Does Leah's journey stir up a story for you? If so, what?

3. What did you learn from listening to Leah?

4. Does Leah's story inspire you to action? If so, what? When? How? Why?

Porch Breezes

Stella spent a brief time in jail, which was her call to change the direction of her life. She knew that she was better than a common druggie even though her cell experience said otherwise. Because this was her first offense, she was given the opportunity to do community service rather spend more time behind bars. The court system allowed Stella to work off her hours by participating in an adult education program so she could earn her GED. And that's when Stella collided with Susannah. Susannah saw the potential in Stella. Susannah's mother-heart would not let Stella slide back. Susannah listened, encouraged, chastised, and loved Stella into successfully completing her GED. Today Stella is living on her own for the first time, rearing her children with love and a tough example of how to succeed, and working toward her master's degree in counseling. She is very clear when she says, "Susannah saved my life!"[8]

> "The Lord will guide you continually, and satisfy your needs in parched places, and make your bones strong; and you shall be like a watered garden, like a spring of water, whose waters never fail" (Isaiah 58:11).

Chapter Five

Rachel—Challenges and Rewards

Genesis 29–31; 35:16–26

Rachel was the daughter of Laban, the second wife of Jacob, and the mother of Joseph and Benjamin.

⚬

I had been the guest of honor all day at a pity party for which I was also the hostess. I do not remember why I was feeling sorry for myself. It might have been that I was forced to handle some problems that day that I did not create. The children might not have called recently. Maybe someone had gotten some new bauble that I had secretly been wanting. Possibly my hair looked like it had been styled with kitchen shears and I felt bloated. For whatever reason, I was feeling as if the world had passed me by and had not even noticed.

I went to the porch to nurse my sore feelings. I was dozing while listening to some music that usually was very soothing to me. Up to that point, the music had been only noise without its normal curative effects. I sighed, and rocked, and sighed some more.

I noticed I was no longer alone. I looked over to the other rocking chair and said to the woman sitting there, "I don't know who you are, but I appreciate your coming to be with me today."

She replied, "You are welcome. My name is Rachel."

"Ah, Rachel, good timing. You've had a life of challenges. Please share with me what you learned."

She reached over, gently patted my arm, and began talking.

"You are right, my sister. Challenge is a good word. When I think back over my life, my first challenge was my father.

"When my future husband, Jacob, came to our home, I was tending the sheep. He saw me and walked over to help with the stone that covered the mouth of the well. We talked as the sheep drank. I fell in love with him then, and he with me. He kissed me, which was very bold of him. I was his from that moment on. I ran home to tell my father that his sister's son, Jacob, was here. My father could tell from the flush in my cheek and the sparkle in my eye that I was interested in this Jacob.

"Before Jacob could reach our house, my father ran out to meet him. Jacob said that his father, Isaac, had sent him to my father to marry one of my father's daughters and to establish himself in the land of Abraham. Jacob worked with my father for a month while they got to know each other.

"Father told Jacob that he wanted to reward him for the work Jacob was doing. He asked Jacob what he would like. Jacob said, 'Rachel.' He agreed to work for my father for seven years so that I could be his wife.

"I was thrilled. As I grew up and matured, I diligently learned all the skills of homemaking in addition to my work with the flocks. Every day I remembered the kiss by the well. I watched Jacob constantly, often without him knowing. When he happened to look up and see my eyes focused on him, he would smile at me. My girlish heart would beat twice as fast as usual as I quickly lowered my eyes.

"Finally the seven long years were up. The wedding preparations kept the entire household in a frenzy. The special foods were prepared, the oil lamps were cleaned and filled, and the guests were invited.

"The evening before the wedding, Father asked me to come to him. I went joyfully, expecting to receive his blessing. But no. He had other ideas. He told me that my older sister, Leah, would be behind the wedding veils instead of me. She was to become Jacob's bride since she was older. I could not believe what my father was saying. How could he do this to me and to Jacob?

"I demanded to know what Jacob thought of this idea. My father informed me that there was no problem with Jacob. I felt betrayed, so betrayed.

"My father suggested that I go the fields so that I would not have to be hurt even more by witnessing my sister's marriage to Jacob. I readily agreed. I did not want to be there for that ultimate insult.

"The next day, I could hear some of the music and laughter as the sound caught on the breezes that fluttered my robe while I watched the sheep graze. It is a good thing that no predator tried to attack the sheep that day, because I would not have seen it. My eyes were too full of tears, and my strength was gone from my weeping.

"I stayed away a couple of nights. When I finally gathered my courage to face the challenge ahead of me, I slowly and reluctantly returned home. The closer I got, the more I could tell that something was not right. I saw Leah at a distance, but she did not look like a well-loved, new bride. My father avoided me altogether. Jacob was nowhere to be seen.

"I grabbed the arm of my maid, Bilhah, as she was walking across the courtyard. I asked her what was going on. She informed me that my father had tricked Jacob into marrying Leah. Jacob had thought all along he was marrying *me*!

"I was furious with my father. How dare he trick my beloved into marrying my sister? How dare he deny me true happiness? How would I ever be able to look my father in the face again? How dare he treat me only as a pawn to serve his own selfish wishes? I hated my father at that moment.

"I stormed into Leah's tent and demanded an explanation of her. She told me she had no idea until the night before the wedding what our father had planned. When I asked her why she went along with this awful situation, she whispered softly, so softly that I hardly heard her, that she too loved Jacob. She knew that this was the only way he could be hers. She started weeping. I fell back onto the pallet where I was sitting. I had no idea of her feeling that way. I was angry with her and yet not angry, because I knew what loving Jacob felt like.

"When she regained some of her composure, she told me there was now a new plan. I rolled my eyes in horror as I tried to guess what next devious idea my father had designed. She said that Jacob would remain with her for the entire marriage week. After that I would be allowed to marry Jacob as well. Our father forced Jacob to commit to working another seven years in return for marrying me.

"Within the course of one week, Jacob ended up with not one wife, but two. Where my reward was to be the wife of Jacob's heart, Leah's reward was to be the mother of his sons. She had three sons within the first three years of their marriage. Then she had a fourth. Still I had no children—girls or boys. What a challenge for me.

"I felt I would die. I complained to Jacob that he was not giving me children. He retorted to me, 'Am I in the place of God, who has withheld from you the fruit of the womb?' (Genesis 30:2). I was beside myself with grief and jealousy. I decided I would give Jacob my maid, Bilhah, so that her children would be my children. Bilhah had two sons with my husband. Then Leah gave Jacob her maid, Zilpah, who bore two more sons. And then, adding insult to insult, Leah gave birth to two more sons. Everywhere I turned, I heard babies crying. None of them cried for me as their mother. I ached inside as I did not know I could ache.

"And then, miracles of miracles, I discovered I was pregnant. The injustices I suffered at my father's hand were wiped away. I was no longer being punished by God for my jealousy for Leah, Bilhah, and Zilpah. I felt I was finally and fully loved by God, my husband, and my son, Joseph. All the challenges I had faced in my life were erased from my mind as I looked on the face of my precious baby boy. Jacob was overwhelmed with joy.

"All the challenges had made me stronger. I more truly appreciated my son because of the loss I had felt prior to his birth. No child was ever more cherished and loved than this one. If I had only known in the beginning that I would be so blessed, my life would have been easier for me. But I could not know. I did not walk in confidence of the love of God.

"One night, Joseph was particularly fussy. I held him close and walked outside, away from our tents. I looked up with my baby in my arms. My Joseph opened the entire night sky for me. Before his birth, I saw the glory of the stars only dimly. After his arrival, the entire sky glistened. If only I could have seen the night lights before, I could have avoided a lot of anger and jealousy. I learned to look up and ponder the wonder of the Lord God and all that is in the world. I learned to delight in the small things of our world when I saw them through Joseph's eyes—the iridescent wings of insects, the way leaves curled, and the swirl of water in a pool. All of my trials were over.

"Eventually, all of us in Jacob's household left my father. My wise husband carefully planned our departure. There was one detail I knew had to be addressed before we were out of the reach of my father. I knew we needed to take what was most precious to him. I am not referring to his daughters or his eleven grandsons and one granddaughter. I'm talking about his household gods. I knew that Father would wheedle and cajole and possibly trick Jacob yet one more time unless I took what he considered to be the source of his power. He searched and searched for those gods. He never found them because I was sitting on them in my camel's saddlebags! At last we were free to become a great nation in our own right.

"We traveled to the land promised to Abraham and Isaac. There I gave birth to Benjamin, and there I died. My family continued and became a great nation that changed the history of the world. Were my challenges worth all that? Most certainly.

"Remember that with challenges come rewards. Go with my blessing."

"Dear Rachel, thank you for sharing with me. My woes are slight compared with yours. Thank you for reminding me of the glories of every moment of life." And with that, she left me alone on the porch.

Rachel's Call to Action

- Look up and ponder the wonder of the Lord God and all that is in the world.

- Delight in the small things of our world.

- Remember that with challenges come rewards.

Your Response to Rachel's Presence

1. Do any of Rachel's calls challenge you in your own life or community? If so, how?

2. Does Rachel's journey stir up a story for you? If so, what?

3. What did you learn from listening to Rachel?

4. Does Rachel's story inspire you to action? If so, what? When? How? Why?

Porch Breezes

> I pray that, according to the riches of his glory, he may grant that you may be strengthened in your inner being with power through his Spirit, and that Christ may dwell in your hearts through faith, as you are being rooted and grounded in love. I pray that you may have the power to comprehend, with all the saints, what is the breadth and length and height and depth, and to know the love of Christ that surpasses knowledge, so that you may be filled with all the fullness of God.
>
> —Ephesians 3:16–19

> "To know what you prefer instead of humbly saying Amen to what the world tells you you ought to prefer, is to have kept your soul alive."[9]

Chapter Six
Shiphrah and Puah—Courage for Doing What Is Right

Exodus 1:15–22

Shiphrah and Puah were midwives during the time the Hebrews were in slavery in Egypt. They disobeyed Pharoah's orders to kill all the Hebrew boy babies.

⎯⫸

People with power were considering decisions that would hurt people I cared about. And yet those responsible for making the decisions were also people who gave substantial sums of money to charitable organizations. It's not that the decision makers were bad people. They were making decisions using the criteria of economic development and not the lens of social justice. I went to the porch to wrestle with the dilemma. I wondered how to make the case for people who were invisible to those with power.

This time reinforcements came. Two women joined me. One sat on either side of me. They each held one of my hands and introduced themselves as Shiphrah and Puah, midwives in ancient Egypt.

I remembered that they, too, had experienced a dilemma to work through. I said, "Hello, Mistress Shiphrah and Mistress Puah. How can I continue the courageous path you opened for me and others?"

They shared with me.

"We are twins, but I suppose you could see that. Even now after all these years, people still have trouble telling us apart. When we speak, we speak with one voice. If you could not see which one of us was moving her lips, you would not know who was speaking.

"When we got that silly edict from Pharoah, we knew without discussing it between ourselves that we were not going to adhere to it. Can you imagine? We are trained midwives. We bring life into the world. We do not take life from this world. What did Pharoah believe when he told us to kill the babies of our own people? He apparently thought of us only as tools for his plans. The edict proved that he did not consider us to be feeling, caring, and wise human beings. We, the Hebrew people, were simply means to his ends. His solution was simple—kill the boys. We giggled when we wondered what Pharoah thought was going to happen in thirteen years when he needed workers for all his hard labor if we indeed killed every one of the boy babies.

"We thought his new law was stupid. But he was the Pharoah. He could kill *us* if he knew what we really thought about his command. We knew we had to be careful.

"We devised our own plan. Whenever a live, male baby was discovered, we would look incredulous, act innocent, and say, 'The Hebrew women are not like the Egyptian women; for they are vigorous and give birth before the midwife comes to them' (Exodus 1:19). And do you know what? The Pharoah was so ignorant of the ways of women, Egyptian and Hebrew, that he believed what we said!

"Since you asked us about our path, we admonish you to look at the laws of the land and consider them carefully. There were some midwives among our people who did as Pharoah ordered simply because he was Pharoah and that was the law of the land. They killed the babies of our own people. They chose to kill innocent babies rather than risk being killed themselves. We could not do that. We had to be disobedient to a bad law. We knew that our God was greater than the voice of Pharoah. We knew that our God honored our lives, and we could not go against our God.

"It was scary when we were questioned about all the boy babies still alive. However, we knew that we followed a higher law. We also knew that a silly law must be seen as a silly law. We had to act accordingly.

"We encourage you to be courageous and stand up for what you know is right—no matter the consequences."

"Wow. You really tell it like it is. Pray that I can share some of your courage." With regret and awe, I realized they had released my hands and gone.

Shiphrah's and Puah's Call to Action

♦   Look at the laws of the land and consider them carefully. See a silly law as a silly law.

♦   Be courageous and stand up for what you know is right—no matter the consequences.

Your Response to Shiphrah's and Puah's Presence

1.   Do any of Shiphrah's and Puah's calls challenge you in your own life or community? If so, how?

2.   Does Shiphrah's and Puah's journey stir up a story for you? If so, what?

3.   What did you learn from listening to Shiphrah and Puah?

4.   Does Shiphrah's and Puah's story inspire you to action? If so, what? When? How? Why?

Porch Breezes

"These forces that threaten to negate life must be challenged by courage, which is the power of life to affirm itself in spite of life's ambiguities. This requires the exercise of a creative will that enables us to hew out a stone of hope from a mountain of despair."[10]

"Wait for the Lord; be strong, and let your heart take courage; wait for the Lord!" (Psalm 27:14)

Stories from the Holocaust and other genocides (*Schindler's List* and *Hotel Rwanda*, for example) inspire us as they tell of people who broke the stated law and thereby saved people's lives.

Chapter Seven

Miriam—Exuberant Celebration and Being Number Two

Exodus 2:1–10; 15; Numbers 12

Miriam watched over her baby brother, Moses, while he was hidden from danger in the bulrushes. When Pharoah's daughter found him, Miriam arranged for their own mother to be his nurse. She worked alongside Moses and her brother, Aaron, when Moses later returned to Egypt to liberate the Hebrew people. After she and the other freed slaves crossed the Red Sea that then swallowed up Pharoah's army, Miriam sang, "Sing to the Lord, for he has triumphed gloriously; horse and rider he has thrown into the sea" (Exodus 15:21). When she and Aaron disapproved of Moses' choice of wife, Miriam was struck with a skin disorder for seven days. During her affliction, given to her by God, the entire group waited in the wilderness for her to heal. Together they journeyed toward the land that was promised.

～ఠ

Jim knows in his deepest parts that his call in life is to be a nurturer and helpmate in the truest sense of the word. He spent extended time with his parents as long as they lived. He nurtures his wife, all his children, their spouses, and his grandchildren in whatever ways they need him to. Often his gentle presence and his naughty sense of humor are all they require. He takes care of all the things that a functioning household needs: meals cooked, yards kept, rooms cleaned, and laundry done.

More than that, he repeatedly says and demonstrates by his actions that he wants to do whatever his wife needs to be able to fulfill her sense of God-given call. Daily he finds ways to make her laugh, because her happiness is paramount to him.

Jim is my husband. I try not to take his loving care for granted, although I'm sure that sometimes I do. My friends are jealous when I talk about the partnership that my husband and I share.

I was on the porch one day and heard Jim working in his shop. The dogs ran in and out from where he was working. I'd watch them run around in the backyard, tussle with each other, and then run back to him. I was thinking how richly blessed I am when I realized that I was not alone.

"Good afternoon. Who are you?"

"I'm Miriam, sister to Moses and Aaron. I'm here to serve you in whatever way I can."

"Hello, Miriam. Sister, from your vast experience, both as slave in Egypt as well as advisor to Moses, what would you have me do to follow your legacy? What do you have to teach me?"

She replied, "You call me sister. That is how I have been known throughout history. I am sister to Moses. My primary role throughout life has been to be secondary—as guide, advisor, and protector of my brother. I confess that I have been prey to what is called 'sibling rivalry.' I was provoked, dare I say jealous, when he married that Cushite woman. Aaron and I both exalted ourselves when we complained aloud that God had spoken through us as well as through Moses. We criticized him for marrying that woman. God chastised us both for challenging Moses, a prophet of God. As a result, I suffered mightily with an irritating and debilitating skin disease. That pain certainly taught me a lesson about challenging Moses and God!

"Most of the time, I was honored to serve in my role as Moses' older sister. Sometimes, however, I did not like being overshadowed by him. Considering that women (and children) were not included in the count of people who wandered those forty years in the wilderness, I'm lucky I was remembered at all. The fact that you know my *name*, Miriam, proves to me that the Holy Lord, Yahweh, valued my part in what became known as the Exodus.

"As a woman, I learned several things that I like to think are valuable for you and others to hold on to. I learned that 'second fiddle,' being in a secondary, supportive role to the person acknowledged as leader, is a vital function. Making sure that Moses was well cared for by our own mother in Pharoah's court was no small feat! Because of me, my brother was able to grow up knowing intimately the ways of Pharoah as well as the beliefs and values of his own Hebrew people. His 'bicultural' heritage became essential as he negotiated with Pharoah, with God's help, for our ultimate release.

"I knew that being second in leadership is an important and honorable calling. I was fully accomplished in my own right. As such, I supported and undergirded the person in charge—Moses, the leader—so he could be much more effective than he ever would have been without my presence, advice, and nurture. Here, of course, I'm speaking in human terms, since we all confess that the Holy God is truly *The Power*!

"My position required being trustworthy and assertive without being threatening or encroaching on the proper authority of the leader. Being able to speak the truth to Moses and not be struck dead was quite a talent! When I forgot that and challenged him about his choice of wife, I suffered the consequences.

"There is a shadow side, though, to the call of second place. Occasionally, I was tempted to deny my own God-giftedness. There are times, I admit, when I played small. Sometimes I believed that I had to reduce myself so that Moses could be large. This, my sister, is *wrong*. Wrong, wrong, wrong.

"However, most of the time I did not try to diminish myself so that Moses could be larger than he already was. In fact, at times I shone. *My words*, 'Sing to the Lord, for he has triumphed gloriously; horse and rider he has thrown into the sea' (Exodus 15:21) are the words that people sing when they tell the story of the crossing of the Red Sea. It is I who helped Moses receive the kind of nurture that Yahweh had planned for him as a child. I, a woman, am remembered in the saga of Moses. My secondary role did *not* mean that I had to make myself smaller so Moses could look large.

"I pray you will remember that being second in leadership is honorable. You must not lose your claim to your God-giftedness in your role.

"On a lighter note, I hope you will sing as I did when we successfully crossed the Red Sea. Sing loudly and joyfully at those times of celebration in life. Sing with enthusiasm. If you cannot sing, then find other ways to be exuberant when life hands you triumph and success. Do not hold back your glee when happiness abounds. Be excessive with your voice and your spirit. Dance, sing, laugh, and make joyful noise. With God's help, you have overcome something. Celebrate and invite everyone around you to join in your exultation. Life is certainly too short not to be extravagant.

"The last thing that I hope you will carry from me is the knowledge that life is indeed a journey. It has turns and hills and valleys. It has obstacles like the Red Sea that seem insurmountable. With God as your guide, you can get through those impossibilities. You may wonder why your path is not straight or why it seems that sometimes you double back rather than make progress. That's simply part of the journey.

"The Lord knows our trip was certainly not easy. We made several wrong turns and disastrous decisions. But in the end, the freed slaves moved into our Land of Promise. Even though I did not actually enter our final destination, what an honor to have been part of the journey!"

"Dear Miriam, thank you for your words of encouragement. You are insightful in ways that have meaning for me. I appreciate your visit." I could hear singing as she went with the breeze.

Miriam's Call to Action

+ Remember that being second in leadership is honorable. Do not lose your claim to your God-giftedness in your role.

+ Sing loudly and joyfully at those times of celebration in life. Sing with enthusiasm. If you cannot sing, then find other ways to be exuberant when life hands you triumph and success. Do not hold back your glee when happiness abounds. Be excessive with your voice and your spirit. Dance, sing, laugh, and make joyful noise.

+ Know that life is indeed a journey.

Your Response to Miriam's Presence

1. Do any of Miriam's calls challenge you in your own life or community? If so, how?

2. Does her journey stir up a story for you? If so, what?

3. What did you learn from listening to Miriam?

4. Does her story inspire you to action? If so, what? When? How? Why?

Porch Breezes

"We believe volunteers are our strength. Who gets credit for a job well done is not as important as realizing that volunteers and staff are all a part of the same team, working for the same goals. We encourage creativity, innovation, and commitment."[11]

When Israel went out from Egypt, the house of Jacob from a people of strange language, Judah became God's sanctuary, Israel his dominion. The sea looked and fled; Jordan turned back. The mountains skipped like rams, the hills like lambs. Why is it, O sea, that you flee? O Jordan, that you turn back? O mountains, that you skip like rams? O hills, like lambs? Tremble, O earth, at the presence of the Lord, at the presence of the God of Jacob, who turns the rock into a pool of water, the flint into a spring of water.

—Psalm 114:1–8

Chapter Eight
Deborah—Resolving Conflict

Judges 4–5

After forty years in the wilderness, Deborah's tribe, Ephraim, along with the other eleven, claimed territories in Canaan. As was the custom, each tribe chose a judge to decide disputes between people. Deborah was her tribe's choice. After she received a vision, she summoned Barak, an Israelite general, to charge him to go to war against King Jabin of Hazor and Sisera, Jabin's commander. When her troops gathered, she prophesied to them, "Up! For this is the day on which the Lord has given Sisera into your hand. The Lord is indeed going out before you" (Judges 4:14). Afterward she sang gloriously of the Israelites' victory and of the demise of Sisera at the hand of Jael, a kinswoman.

For some reason, congregations seem to be fertile fields for conflict. Church conflicts seem to revolve around a few themes:

1. The old way of doing things versus the new way;

2. Interpersonal conflict with the minister that might include misconduct;

3. Finances;

4.   Who has the right to make decisions and orders regarding the congregation's life.

The conflict resolution team that I was a member of attended several meetings to listen to the congregation's affirmations and complaints and to make suggestions to the ruling body of the congregation for how to proceed. For the most part, the process was experienced as healing, if not pleasant. I was rocking on the porch, trying to gather my thoughts before leaving for what might be the final meeting with the group.

I was joined by Deborah. After she introduced herself, I said, "Hello, Deborah. Powerful woman, what is your call to me? What work of yours do I need to carry on?"

She advised me by saying, "Worthy woman, need you ask? My divine call was to mediate among my people. Of course, I led Barak into battle and defeated Jabin, king of Hazor, which is primarily why history remembers me. However, my main task, the focus of my life, was to resolve conflict. I settled disputes while sitting under a palm tree located between Ramah and Bethel.

"For some reason, the people who came to me for judgment or for mediation seemed determined to tell me how to solve their dispute. They had already decided who the enemy was, and it was not them! They hoped I would choose for one and crush the other. I, on the other hand, hoped that both parties would gain from my decision. When the fighting words and emotions continued and became really negative, some people wanted me to eliminate totally the offending party. This was not good.

"I knew that conflict happened whenever more than one person was in a gathering. I also knew that conflict could be healthy. As a judge, I tried to help people learn and develop skills that could help them successfully manage their disputes. I encouraged them to stay focused on their relationship with the Holy God rather than on demolishing others. I required that a person speak only for himself or herself. When someone came to me and repeated what 'others are saying,' I dismissed that one. When people involved in a dispute called each other names, I refused to render a judgment. I focused on the issues rather than the personalities of the people involved.

"I was fully aware that there was not just one way to solve conflicts.

Indeed, the process of discerning required wisdom, patience, and a non-anxious presence grounded in divine wisdom.

"Our God is about harmonious and mutually nurturing relationships. My job was to ensure that the conflict was resolved in a healthy and positive way. My call to mediate and judge was from God. By listening for God's guidance, I was able to discern the questions to ask and the advice to offer. Beyond that, the situation was out of my hands and rested only within our loving and compassionate God, our ultimate judge. When people did not come to me for my judgment and chose instead to fight among themselves, they demonstrated that they thought they knew better than God what and who was right.

"I was aware that when I offered my decision, some liked it. Others did not. A few took their disappointment or anger out on me. Others, of course, exalted me and put me in the place that is reserved only for the Lord God Almighty. I struggled to remember always that I was God's servant and that the anger and the praise really had nothing to do with me personally. I simply pulled from the wisdom of the Creator and spoke the words that needed to be said. The Lord God enabled me to render my decisions dispassionately, with little or no anxiety, and with no investment in what the people ultimately chose to do with my words and guidance. That choice was in God's hands.

"By helping people settle their disputes, I earned and enjoyed trust and respect. If this is your call, take this responsibility and opportunity as the wonderful gift from God that it is for you and for the people who receive this gift from you. Honor God as you use it.

"I charge you to find your tree under which to work."

"Dear Judge Deborah, your wisdom will go with me into this meeting and all others where conflict is an issue. Thank you." I believe I heard marching steps as she vanished from the porch.

Deborah's Call to Action

- If helping deal with conflict is your call, take this responsibility and opportunity as the wonderful gift from God that it is for you and for the people who receive this gift from you. Honor God as you use it.

+ Find your tree under which to work.

Your Response to Deborah's Presence

1. Do any of Deborah's calls challenge you in your own life or community? If so, how?

2. Does Deborah's journey stir up a story for you? If so, what?

3. What did you learn from listening to Deborah?

4. Does Deborah's story inspire you to action? If so, what? When? How? Why?

Porch Breezes

"The moral aim for Christian parties to a conflict is self-investment in the good with others rather than self-sacrifice for the good of others."[12]

"In the fear of not being loved by God, we spend a lot of our energy and time enforcing the rules that we set for ourselves by thinking they are God's rules."[13]

Chapter Nine
Levite's Concubine—Abuse and Sacrifice

Judges 19

A concubine belonged to a Levite priest. After he reclaimed her from Bethlehem, where she had escaped to her father's house, the Levite began the return journey with her to the hill country of Ephraim. He stopped at night in Gibeah, seeking shelter. An old field worker invited the travelers to his home. During the night, the men of Gibeah, from the tribe of Benjamin, demanded the priest come out of the house so they could torment and humiliate him. His concubine was forced to take his place. She was gang raped and died as a result. Her master took her mutilated body home. He hacked her body into twelve pieces that he sent to the other tribes as a call to civil war against the tribe of Benjamin.

Sometime the woes of the world feel overwhelming. Newscasts talk about increasing numbers of murders or war deaths and show pictures of genocide or starvation. A woman who was abused as a child is charged with abusing her own children. People are paid cash "under the table" so the employer does not have to pay fair wages or provide benefits to which the worker is entitled. Adults scream at children, calling them "stupid" or saying, "I wish you were dead!" Evidence of sexism, racism, classism, and ageism abounds.

I feel powerless in the face of such devastating actions. There are times when I cannot be involved in the world because of all the pain and damage that I witness. I must retreat to get perspective on what I *can* do, what I *can* help to address, and where I *can* spend my energy. If I can't go to the mountains that consistently nurture my soul, then I retreat to the porch.

I had come to expect words of encouragement, insight, or inspiration from the women who came to rock with me. Never did I expect one of the victims of humanity's abuse to appear. But she came. I do not even know her name. She looked at me through eyes that were painful to peer into. I saw the damage that was evident on her body and said, "Hello. Please tell me, wounded woman, what is your request of me? How can I honor your life?"

She spoke softly with her eyes downcast. I could hardly hear what she said at first. She whispered. "Please put me back together. I do not mean gather my body parts and sew them each to the other, even if that were possible. I want to be re-membered.

"My life was never my own. I was under the control of my father, then my master, then that so-called host, and finally those thugs. I was taken as a concubine from my father's house in Bethlehem. I was not even given the status of wife. I wept and wept at my fate. I managed to get away from my master's house, but I had nowhere to go except to return to my father.

"After four months, my master came for me. My father was overjoyed when my master appeared to reclaim me. My father called my master 'son-in-law.' I was embarrassed. My father acted as if I were the bride of my master. My father fawned all over him, feeding him and enticing him to stay day after day.

"'Father, Father! He is not my husband! He is my master!' I wanted to scream.

"My mother tried to help me see my plight in a positive way. She reminded me of the price my master had paid my father for me to be his concubine. Of *course* my father was thrilled to see my master. He hoped to cajole more livestock and money from my master in exchange for my return.

"All too soon for me, we left. I left my childhood home once again to return to the remote hill country. Since we could not make the trip in one day, we had to seek shelter in Gibeah. My master sat in the square, waiting for someone to offer us hospitality for the night. A field worker, returning home for the evening, finally took us in.

"I can hardly speak the rest of my story. Men came in the night, asking for my master so they could rape him. Instead, my master threw me out to them. They raped me repeatedly. They tortured me. They mutilated me. They left me for dead at the closed door of the house.

"Meanwhile my master slept—safe in his bed.

"I gave my life for this man. I did not choose to be with him and I did not willingly die for him. But I did give my life.

"What I ask of you is to protect vulnerable people who are forced to give up their lives to those with power. Some people may not have to literally give their lives for others as I did, but they may give up their health, their emotional well-being, their dreams, or their own families. That is what I had already done even before I was thrown out of the door into the night.

"Can you believe that some people say I deserved what I got? I was without a name or voice or control of my life. What happened to me is a graphic description of what happens every day—rape of spirit, rape of spiritual life, rape of body, rape of soul, rape of land, and rape of other species.

"After the rape and my death, I was dismembered and used to stir up civil war. I did not even receive a proper burial. My human body was not honored once again. I became only a thing, an invitation, a commodity to be used by men who thirsted for power, revenge, and control. I was simply a pawn.

"Please, I beg you, stop people from using others as pawns for their own ambitions. My death was used as an excuse for thousands of other killings, both of Israelites and Benjaminites. This ongoing killing was not a way to honor my life. But of course they knew that. My life to them had no honor. So why did they call for war to honor my death?

"They did not want to honor me. They wanted revenge for my master's poor treatment in Gibeah. They sought recompense for the destruction of his property, me, by kinsmen who should have honored him rather than humiliated him. In their greed, they wanted more.

"Please re-member me and all those like me. Honor our lives. Honor our deaths. Honor us with no more killing. Honor us by working to end the violation of people's spirits and souls. Re-member me. I gave my life for another. That was a holy gift. Honor my sacrifice as you honor the Christ who also gave his life."

"Oh, my dear, sweet sister, how I hurt for you. I do want to re-member you. Thank you for sharing this painful story." With regret, I realized that she had disappeared and was once more invisible.

The Concubine's Call to Action

- Protect vulnerable people who are forced to give up their lives to those with power.

- Stop people from using others as pawns for their own ambitions.

- Re-member me and all those like me. Honor our lives. Honor our deaths. Honor us with no more killing. Honor us by working to end the violation of people's spirits and souls. Re-member me.

Your Response to the Concubine's Presence

1. Do any of this woman's calls challenge you in your own life or community? If so, how?

2. Does the Concubine's journey stir up a story for you? If so, what?

3. What did you learn from listening to the Concubine's story?

4. Does her story inspire you to action? If so, what? When? How? Why?

Porch Breezes

Currently, the best estimate of the incidence and prevalence of rape is provided by the National Violence Against Women study, published in 2000 and sponsored by the National Institute of Justice and the Centers for Disease

Control. This study employed a sampling strategy that closely matched national demographics and found the following:

♦ 14.8% of women were victims of rape at some point during their lifetime;

♦ 2.8% of women were victims of attempted rape at some point during their lifetime;

♦ 0.3% of women were victims of rape during the previous 12 months, yielding an 8.7 per 1000 "incidence rate."

Extrapolating this incidence rate to the population of Metro Boston reveals the stark disparity between "official" rape statistics and the reality of sexual violence. In 1998, there were 1,687 rapes reported in all of Massachusetts, and 526 arrests were made. That same year, among the approximately 1.75 million women in the Boston Metro area, there were actually 15,225 rapes.[14]

Deliver me, O Lord, from evildoers; protect me from those who are violent, who plan evil things in their minds and stir up wars continually. They make their tongue sharp as a snake's, and under their lips is the venom of vipers. Guard me, O Lord, from the hands of the wicked; protect me from the violent who have planned my downfall. The arrogant have hidden a trap for me, and with cords they have spread a net, along the road they have set snares for me ... I know that the Lord maintains the cause of the needy, and executes justice for the poor. Surely the righteous shall give thanks to your name; the upright shall live in your presence.

—Psalm 140:1–5, 12–13

Chapter Ten
Hannah—Yearning and Promises

1 Samuel 1:1–2:11; 2:18–21

Hannah was the wife of Elkanah and the mother of Samuel and his brothers and sisters. She was childless when she went to Shiloh with her husband to pray for a son. The priest, Eli, thought she was drunk when he heard her agitated prayers. When she corrected him by telling him she was pouring out her soul to the Lord, he said, "Go in peace; the God of Israel grant the petition you have made to him" (1Samuel 1:17). She went home and became pregnant with Samuel. Her son became a prophet and a kingmaker.

Julia Child was an inspiration to many, and not just because she could cook. People also admired her because she came into her professional persona in her mid-fifties. She was not one of the teen actor or musician success stories who struggle to stay young, cute, and perky for as long as possible. No, Julia Child was the antithesis of celebrity. She was not particularly attractive. Her voice was one to be mocked. And she was considered old by today's standards of when people "come into their own." But people loved her. She taught multitudes how to cook elegant and nutritious meals and have fun doing it. We appreciated her and mourned when she died.

We are lucky when, as young women, we have older women who are willing to mentor us. They share the skills they have, the insights they have gleaned, and the esteem in which they are held.

As I got older, I began to wonder when and if God was going to open that "Julia Child Door" for me. I questioned if my experiences would have wisdom for anyone else or if I would simply plug away until death's door (not Julia Child's) opened for me.

I was thinking about the wisdom of age and experience while I sipped a glass of tea on the porch. Slowly, I heard singing becoming louder and louder from a voice that sounded old. I finally could make out these words, "My heart exults in the Lord."

I asked the voice, "What is that you are singing?"

The voice became embodied in a woman, who answered as she settled into the rocking chair, "I'm singing my song. I am Hannah."

"Hello, Mother Hannah. Please, what wisdom will you share with me? What are you calling me to do?"

She hummed another line or two of her song and said, "I am a woman richly blessed, even though for years I did not think I was. My husband, Elkanah, loved me dearly. But Peninnah, another wife to my husband, was the mother of my husband's children and she never let me forget it.

"I wanted a child more than life itself. I prayed and prayed and prayed. I finally told the Lord that if I could have a baby boy, I'd lend that bundle of blessedness to the Lord as soon as the child was weaned. And that is exactly what happened! God gave me Samuel.

"On the day that Elkanah and I took our son to Eli at Shiloh, I was both tearful and joyful. I was sad that I could not see my precious child every day and that I could not feed him from my own table. I was glad that the Lord had given him to me and proud that my precious Samuel could serve this loving and giving Lord. My heart was full and my thoughts were chaotic.

"So what do I call you to do?

"Let's see. I call you to bring to the Lord your deepest heart yearnings. At times you may not, cannot, or will not claim what has been laid on your heart by our Lord. Our God created you, my child, and you may sometimes forget that. Remember that I did not choose to settle, to live in a limited way, or to deny the desires that the Lord placed in me at my very creation.

"I know I was tempted to listen to the voice of my beloved husband. I loved him and I valued his opinion. But he was not God in my life. My dear, sweet Elkanah would try to make me feel better by saying, 'Hannah, why do you weep? Why do you not eat? Why is your heart sad? Am I not more to you than ten sons?' (1 Samuel 1:8). Then he would say, 'I love you twice as much as I love Peninnah. What more do you need? Don't cry. Don't seek for something you cannot have. Don't feel bad.' He thought his words, intended to comfort me, would take away my grief.

"I know he thought he was helping me. I know he thought he was loving me—and he was, the best way he knew. But when he told me how much he loved me and asked me not to feel sad, I felt … I felt discounted. I felt as if my feelings were not important. And then I felt guilty because my husband did truly love me. I simply felt that he did not *really* know me in the deepest parts of my being.

"But Peninnah did. She knew what I most deeply wanted. She taunted me with it. My nemesis, my adversary, my rival prodded me. She pushed me.

"Today I can be grateful to her. 'Grateful?' you ask incredulously. Yes, grateful. Had she not kept nagging me, I would not have realized my deepest purpose. I would not have prayed and prayed to the Lord to give me a baby. I would not have been thought drunk because I was pouring out my heart. Who knows? Without Peninnah's taunts, I may never have had my Samuel, the kingmaker for both King Saul and King David.

"Peninnah helped me claim what my loving husband could not. I challenge you to listen to the voices that help you claim the yearnings God has placed in your heart. Occasionally those voices may come from people who antagonize rather than love you.

"I charge you as well to honor your commitments. I told the Lord that if only the Holy God would give me a baby boy, then I would set my son before the Lord as a nazarite. I kept my pledge.

"I have to be honest with you. After I saw that sweet face and smelled his unmistakable baby smells and touched his soft skin, I was sorely tempted to refuse to honor my pledge. I began to think that maybe I had been mistaken, that surely the Lord would understand, and that I could keep this precious child. Even as I tried to convince myself that my pledge did not mean anything, though, I knew otherwise.

"As I look back, I now know without any hesitation that keeping my pledge was God's plan. Just look at Samuel's life and how he changed the history of Israel, and you too will know. I charge you again to keep your commitments. Honor your word. Being trustworthy is a powerful way to honor God.

"When I returned home after leaving Samuel with Eli at Shiloh, I prayed to the Lord again. This time I was full of praise and not petition. I could finally understand and sing about how our Lord provides for all of us. 'The bows of the mighty are broken, but the feeble gird on strength' (1 Samuel 2:4). God blessed me with other children! I realized that everything is under God's gracious care: those who have children and those who do not, those who are hungry and those who are not, those who are dying and those who are living. I sang about being faithful and about God's judgment. In the end, I claimed a blessing for my dear son when I sang, 'The Lord will … exalt the power of his anointed' (1 Samuel 2:10).

"That God certainly did through my Samuel!

"I ask you to carry on my work. Help people acknowledge that everything depends on God: success, failure, power, weakness, love, and judgment. Help people claim their deepest yearnings that were planted inside them by God. Sing my song and teach others the words as well. There is no Holy God like the Lord! And then always, always honor your promises to God."

"Mother Hannah, I celebrate with you. Thank you for sharing your wisdom." In just moments, I was once again alone with only the buzzing bees for companions.

Hannah's Call to Action

+ Listen to the voices that help you claim the yearnings God has placed in your heart, even when those voices may come from people who antagonize rather than love you.

+ Keep your commitments.

+ Honor your word. Being trustworthy is a powerful way to honor God.

- Help people acknowledge that everything depends on God: success, failure, power, weakness, love, and judgment.

- Help people claim their deepest yearnings that were planted inside them by God.

- Sing my song and teach others the words as well.

- Always, always honor your promises to God.

Your Response to Hannah's Presence

1. Do any of Hannah's calls challenge you in your own life or community? If so, how?

2. Does her journey stir up a story for you? If so, what?

3. What did you learn from listening to Hannah?

4. Does her story inspire you to action? If so, what? When? How? Why?

Porch Breezes

The words to Hannah's song are:

> My heart exults in the Lord; my strength is exalted in my God. My mouth derides my enemies, because I rejoice in my victory. "There is no Holy One like the Lord, no one besides you; there is no Rock like our God. Talk no more so very proudly, let not arrogance come from your mouth; for the Lord is a God of knowledge, and by him actions are weighed. The bows of the mighty are broken, but the feeble gird on strength. Those who were full have hired themselves out for bread, but those who were hungry are fat with spoil. The barren has borne seven, but she who has many children is forlorn. The Lord kills and brings to life; he brings down to Sheol and raises up. The Lord makes poor and makes rich; he brings low, he also exalts.

He raises up the poor from the dust; he lifts the needy from the ash heap, to make them sit with princes and inherit a seat of honor. For the pillars of the earth are the Lord's, and on them he has set the world. He will guard the feet of his faithful ones, but the wicked shall be cut off in darkness; for not by might does one prevail. The Lord! His adversaries shall be shattered; the Most High will thunder in heaven. The Lord will judge the ends of the earth; he will give strength to his king, and exalt the power of his anointed."

—1 Samuel 2:1–10

Chapter Eleven

Bathsheba—Authority and Nurture

2 Samuel 11:1–26; 12:15–25; 1 Kings 1:1–40; 2:1–25

Bathsheba was married twice—first to Uriah and then to David, the king. She gave birth to two children, one who died when only seven days old and the second, a son named Solomon, who succeeded his father, David, to the throne. Solomon was known for his wisdom.

The words "I'm pregnant" can be the most joyous words ever heard or the most devastating. They have the power to change the history of a family or a nation. My next visitor to the porch reinforced for me the power of those words.

Bathsheba joined me one afternoon shortly after a colleague exuberantly announced she was going to be a grandmother. After introducing herself (although her regal clothes and bearing led me to assume she must be Bathsheba), I said, "Hello, Queen Mother. What would you have me learn from your journey? What words of wisdom do you have to impart?"

Here is her story:

"History has cast me in the role of manipulative woman. I have considered this label and admit my confusion. I really do not know if I was a manipulator or not. Yes, I was bathing as part of my ritual purification. Did I know that I could be seen from the roof of the king's house? I honestly cannot say whether I knew that or not. My husband, an honorable and upright soldier, was often away. I admit I was lonely.

"When the king saw me, he sent for me. I, of course, did what he said. After all, to refuse the king might have meant my death. I was both thrilled and dismayed to have been chosen by the king for his special favors. I honored Uriah, my husband, and still I wanted to be the king's special wife. Did I entice David? I do not think so, but I am no longer sure of my motives. So much has happened since that fateful interchange.

"When I realized that I was pregnant, I did not know what to do. The only thing I could think of was to notify the king. I could have been stoned for adultery when my condition became known. All my acquaintances knew that Uriah was serving the king in battle so they would have guessed he was not the father of the child I was carrying. David ordered Uriah to come home from his military service in order to try to provide a cover for my pregnancy. However, my husband, honorable soldier that he was, refused to pleasure himself with me while his comrades were still in battle.

"What happened next has caused me numerous sleepless nights. Uriah was ordered to the front lines and was killed. After an appropriate time of mourning, I became another of David's wives—but his favorite!

"I have learned some things from all that experience. When someone in authority tells you to do something that you know in your heart is wrong, think twice. No, think more than twice. Think about it five times; no, ten times. I felt that I had no options. Maybe I did and maybe I did not. I do not know what would have happened if I had refused the king's attention. I do know that Uriah might still be alive.

"I admit that I did not use the intelligence God gave me. I acquiesced to power. I am not proud of that fact. And yet, I realize that I might do the same thing again. My fear of death, my training to always obey any man in my life, my loneliness, my allegiance to the king, and my sense of powerlessness in the face of such power led me to enter the king's chambers when he bid me to come. I became his wife and bore his children.

"My firstborn child died. It seems the sins of the father are indeed visited upon the next generation. And yet I know that God is a gracious God and can redeem situations that seem unredeemable. I know this because of my next child, my son, Solomon.

"Even though I have confusion and, yes, guilt, about my role in Uriah's death, I have no regrets about being Solomon's mother. David had promised that our son would become his successor. There were several attempts to steal the throne away from Solomon, but finally, with some pressure from me and the prophet Nathan, David declared Solomon to be next in line for his throne.

"I gave birth to the man who has been known throughout the ages for being wise. My contribution to the world was that I taught my son to think. My son learned to listen to the voice of God and to love the Holy One. I taught my son about justice, mercy, and leadership. I challenged him to be a fine human being. I never belittled him, never called him stupid or challenged his abilities. He had opportunities to glow with his God-given light. Solomon was raised to be king. I knew that God had chosen my son for greatness.

"I caution you to trust your own intelligence when it comes to making decisions large and small. I urge you to do whatever it takes to nurture children to grow into their God-given lives."

"Mother Bathsheba, you give thoughtful words of advice. Thank you." When she left, I knew that I had been in the presence of a queen.

Bathsheba's Call to Action

- When someone in authority tells you to do something which you know in your heart is wrong, think twice. No, think more than twice. Think about it five times; no, ten times.

- Trust your own intelligence when it comes to making decisions large and small.

- Do whatever it takes to nurture children to grow into their God-given lives.

Your Response to Bathsheba's Presence

1. Do any of Bathsheba's calls challenge you in your own life or community? If so, how?

2. Does her journey stir up a story for you? If so, what?

3. What did you learn from listening to Bathsheba?

4. Does her story inspire you to action? If so, what? When? How? Why?

Porch Breezes

"God of choice, sometimes something comes our way that flatters our innermost being. Someone gives us the opportunity to be bigger, more important, or more powerful. And yet, how do we know this is a gift from you? You have given us choice but not always laced that option with clarity. Is that part of listening more closely to you? To leaning more on you? If this is of you, make it stronger. If not, let it weaken and lose its fascination. Amen"[15]

[Integrity is a journey toward completeness. Elements in the journey include:] "1) discerning what is right and wrong, 2) acting on what you have discerned, even at personal cost, and 3) saying openly that you are acting on your understanding of right from wrong."[16]

For this reason, since the day we heard it, we have not ceased praying for you and asking that you may be filled with the knowledge of God's will in all spiritual wisdom and understanding, so that you may lead lives worthy of the Lord, fully pleasing to him, as you bear fruit in every good work and as you grow in the knowledge of God. May you be made strong with all the strength that comes from his glorious power, and may you be prepared to endure everything with patience, while joyfully giving thanks to the Father, who has enabled you to share in the inheritance of the saints in the light.

—Colossians 1:9–12

Chapter Twelve
Tamar—Victimization and Accountability

2 Samuel 13

Tamar thought she was ministering to her brother, Amnon, who pretended to be sick. Instead she walked into a trap that enabled him to rape her. Tamar's father, King David, inadvertently aided Amnon by honoring his son's request to have her come feed him. After the vile deed, when Amnon cast her aside, her father once again caused her harm by ignoring Amnon's actions. Tamar's brother, Absalom, took her in and avenged her betrayal.

She knew what he had said to her was inappropriate for a minister to say. When she overheard him say something with sexual overtones to another female, she convinced herself that she had to report him to the church authorities. She wrote a letter, outlining what had been said and when.

If she thought she had been living in a nightmare before, she was mistaken. The nightmare escalated even more when her letter became public in the congregation. She was accused of attacking a beloved minister. People treated her as if she had a highly contagious disease. She was thought to be mentally and emotionally unstable. Her spirit was raped by the people in the congregation where she had grown up and where her faith life had been nurtured. A long journey of pain, anger, and ultimately healing began.

Nevertheless, occasionally something from that long-ago event still catches her off guard, and the tears and pain surface.

She and I had communicated via e-mail that day. Later, in the early evening, I was still processing our dialogue when Tamar appeared on the porch. After I knew who my companion was, I asked, "Tamar, wounded sister, what are you calling me to do?"

She replied, "What am I calling you to do? I'm calling you to stop the sexual violation of anyone. Is that clear enough? It happens everywhere. It really angers me when women are used by men and then are blamed for their very victimization.

"Let me explain. I heard rumors among the court servants that Amnon had accused me of seducing him. He said that I came to him and made cakes for him. That is true. He said I willingly went into his bedchambers to feed the cakes to him. That also is true. He requested that I do both. I thought nothing of honoring the requests of my brother. He, on the other hand, made my actions sound vile.

"I did those things, but at the request of my brother, who I thought was ill. I was, I have to admit, honored by the attention of my brother, since he was the firstborn of my father. I trusted him. After all, he was my brother. Then he used his power and my vulnerability for his own sexual gratification.

"Amnon's actions certainly demonstrated that he was about power, not love. He thought he loved me. But he violated the rules of conduct when he forced me to lie with him. He violated my trust, and he violated me. As soon as he'd satisfied his craving by exerting power over me, he hated me! He pushed me away. He threw me away. He went on as if nothing had happened!

"My father, the king, *The Power*, allowed him to get away with it. The king chose his son over me, his daughter. My father—the person I most revered in the whole world—sided with Amnon in this heinous act. My father's willingness to ignore my pain, to pretend that I and my feelings did not exist, to blame me for what happened, and to label *me* as a fallen woman stabbed me to the very core. My father, King David, the power in my life and the one who could make things right again, refused to help me.

What Amnon had done to me began to pale in comparison with what my father did to me.

"Will you, for my sake, stand with the victims of sexual malfeasance and misconduct? Will you help women know that they were used and abused by the powers that surrounded them? Will you help them see that men violate their trust and their personhood when men use them for sexual gratification? And that this is true even if the woman went to her assailant willingly and maybe for very honorable reasons?

"Will you also call the powers of the world to accountability? Just because someone has status, prestige, or power with words does not mean that he should be allowed to get away with his abuse. Demand that the authorities, the powers, require him to acknowledge the damage he has done. Insist that he feel some of the pain, betrayal, and hurt he has caused to women like me.

"I suffered the shame and degradation of what happened to me for my entire life. My dear brother Absalom took me in. He eventually killed Amnon for what Amnon did to me. That action caused even more damage in my family. The violence went on and on because it was not handled when it first happened. My father, the *king*, did not say forcefully and vehemently to Amnon, 'Guilty.' Therefore the violence and the damage continued.

"My sister, feel my pain. Acknowledge my situation. Vindicate me by changing the systems that allow abusers of women—and power—to remain free of responsibility and accountability for their actions. Speak for all the Tamars. Challenge the Amnons and King Davids. You asked what I call you to do? This is it."

"Tamar, your passionate pleas cannot be ignored. Help all of us to honor your challenges." As I looked off in the distance to think about Tamar's plight, she said good-bye. Her final words were, "Don't forget."

Tamar's Call to Action

- Stand with the victims of sexual malfeasance and misconduct.

- Help them know that they were used and abused by the powers that surrounded them.

- Help them see that men violated their trust and their personhood when men used them for sexual gratification, even if the woman went to her assailant willingly and maybe for very honorable reasons.

- Call the powers of the world to accountability.

- Demand that the authorities, the powers, require him to acknowledge the damage he has done. Insist that he feel some of the pain, betrayal, and hurt he caused to women like me.

- Feel my pain. Acknowledge my situation. Vindicate me by changing the systems that allow abusers of women—and power—to remain free of responsibility and accountability for their actions.

- Speak for all the Tamars. Challenge the Amnons and King Davids.

Your Response to Tamar's Presence

1. Do any of Tamar's calls challenge you in your own life or community? If so, how?

2. Does Tamar's journey stir up a story for you? If so, what?

3. What did you learn from listening to Tamar?

4. Does Tamar's story inspire you to action? If so, what? When? How? Why?

Porch Breezes

"Do not fear, for I am with you, do not be afraid, for I am your God; I will strengthen you, I will help you, I will uphold you with my victorious right hand" (Isaiah 41:10).

Tamar's Voice is a religious nonprofit organization. "We are here to listen and encourage those who have been sexually abused by members of the clergy." The objectives are: "to promote healing for those affected by pastoral misconduct; reach out in grace, truth, and love; listen to people who need to tell their story; empower the voiceless to speak out; encourage integrity in ministerial relationships."[17]

Chapter Thirteen

Huldah—Trusting and Speaking God's Truth

2 Kings 22:1–23:30

Huldah's validation of the Scriptures led to national reform. As a prophet, she was not in the official religious establishment. She was divinely recruited by God. Huldah is remembered for her knowledge of Scripture and for having the courage to interpret Scripture for a king. She began the process of defining and claiming which holy writings were of God.

"Authorities" disagree about many things. They use resources that support their particular stance while others, just as authoritative, quote research that supports opposite conclusions. It can all be very confusing.

While sitting on the porch, I was pondering the many "authorities" who disagree with each other on the same topic, whatever that topic may be. It seems that the truth is not always what the majority says. I was wondering how to discern which authority speaks the truth among the many other truths that are evident at the moment. How does one hear the voice of God among the cacophony of rhetoric?

On this day, I was joined on the porch by Huldah. I immediately recognized her because I had seen a quilt made by internationally known fabric artist, Penny Sisto, with Huldah's face in the center. Huldah was beautiful, with milk-chocolate skin. On her forehead was a faint star. Her presence exuded faith and assurance.

"Hello, Huldah. Your eyes see what others cannot. You are specially chosen by God. You are confident and faithful. What are you calling me to do?"

She began, "Child, listen to me. I was given a gift—one I did not even especially want. But gifted I was. My gift set me apart in ways both good and bad. A king sought my counsel, but women isolated me. What could I do except follow that inner knowing? That inner conviction?

"Yes, I could see, feel, and know what others could not. The ruler, King Josiah, recognized my knowing and my integrity. I guess that he and his priests knew of me and my gift through my husband, Shallum, who was the keeper of the wardrobe. The king knew I spoke from a place deep inside me, even deeper than the depths of our native soil.

"When I was younger, I questioned this knowing. And yet, time and time again, my knowing enriched me and others. My knowing helped change lives, certainly my own but also the lives of others. When the Holy Lord comes close, believe me, things happen!

"I could see a path that was laid out by God. I was pushed from behind by this God. I was pulled from the front by this God. I was carried by this God when I could not continue along the path. I was accompanied by this God.

"So when the God-appointed time came that the king needed answers from God, God gave me the opportunity to speak the truth. I was presented with long-lost documents that told us how to live and told us what the God of ancient Israel wanted from us. People thought I was out of step with reality, since I did not go along with all the hoopla that passed for religion in those days. I listened in my heart to the one true God, the one of the stories that were still told in the evenings, sitting around the table.

"The God of those stories had grabbed my heart and my mind. I was touched by this God. Every moment of my life confirmed that this God was the true reality—not all the realities that the people claimed in their loose living and lack of compassion, and certainly not in their worship of all those other gods! I said the documents that the workers had found during the renovations of the house of the Lord were of God.

"Now you ask me how I want you to carry on my legacy? How do I want you to continue along the path that God has prepared? Trust the insight and wisdom that God has placed in your heart and mind. Your knowing is a sacred gift. Treasure it and nurture it. You may not have wisdom that will turn around a nation—but then again, maybe you do.

"Do not be persuaded by your friends and family to listen to other voices. Only the Holy God speaks true. Have courage, little one. When God's hand is on you, you are not alone. You are tapped into a wellspring of wisdom and insight and compassion that others need and will seek out.

"Speak God's truth. Speak what you know from your preparation in listening to God. Speak, knowing that others will discount you, ignore you, and place derogatory labels on you. But remember, those other people are not the keepers of your soul, the guides for your life, or the sustainers of your spirit.

"Look at me. A whole lot of people scorned me and derided me. They are long dead and no one remembers them. But you know my name and you know what I did. I live. I live to share with you what I have learned. I live to challenge you in your journey. I live to walk with you, calling you to confidence and fidelity to what you know.

"Listen, speak, have courage, and you will continue what I began. I love you, child. Go with God's and my blessings. Dearest one, I spoke to a king. To whom will you speak?"

"Most honorable Huldah, you say true words that speak to my heart. Thank you." I reluctantly watched her dignified leave-taking.

Huldah's Call to Action

- Trust the insight and wisdom that God has placed in your heart and mind. Your knowing is a sacred gift. Treasure it and nurture it.

- Do not be persuaded by your friends and family to listen to other voices. Only the Holy God speaks true. Have courage, little one.

+ Speak God's truth. Speak what you know from your preparation in listening to God. Speak, knowing that others will discount you, ignore you, and place derogatory labels on you.

+ Listen, speak, have courage, and you will continue what I began.

Your Response to Huldah's Presence

1. Do any of Huldah's calls challenge you in your own life or community? If so, how?

2. Does her journey stir up a story for you? If so, what?

3. What did you learn from listening to Huldah?

4. Does her story inspire you to action? If so, what? When? How? Why?

Porch Breezes

"The fear of the Lord is the beginning of wisdom; all those who practice it have a good understanding. His praise endures forever" (Psalm 111:10).

"You must train your intuition—you may trust the small voice inside you which tells you exactly what to say, what to decide."[18]

"Let the word of Christ dwell in you richly; teach and admonish one another in all wisdom; and with gratitude in your hearts sing psalms, hymns, and spiritual songs to God. And whatever you do, in word or deed, do everything in the name of the Lord Jesus, giving thanks to God the Father through him" (Colossians 3:16–17).

Chapter Fourteen
Naomi—Perseverance and God's Goodness

Book of Ruth

Naomi and her daughter-in-law, Ruth, returned to Bethlehem, Naomi's hometown, after the death of Naomi's husband, Elimelech, and Naomi's sons sons, one of whom was Ruth's husband. There, Naomi orchestrated Ruth's marriage to Boaz, her kinsman.

After years of struggle to keep our marriage together, the father of my sons and I realized that there was no longer anything to save. I began looking at my past, my present, and my future through new lenses. I had stunted my own growth for a long time because I felt that was what was necessary to keep my marriage together. That attitude now gave way to flourishing change and new vistas. I constantly was amazed and surprised as I learned new ways of interacting with other people, as my creativity was reborn, and as I relaxed in fresh and youth-energizing ways. After a time, I married the man I intend to spend the rest of my life with. He continues to help me let go of the painful past and find the peace to reclaim the positive lessons and events of that former time.

Nevertheless, on marker dates, I continued to return to review the divorce event that was totally life-changing for me. On one anniversary date of my first wedding, I was sitting on the porch with eyes moist from memories of the loss and the overwhelming sense of failure I had experienced. I felt arms surround me from behind my chair. Although I couldn't see who had joined me, I leaned back and felt soothed by that loving touch. I did not want to break the spell of being totally nurtured, so I waited. As she released me from her warm embrace, she spoke. "I am Naomi."

"Hello, Naomi. You have suffered a lot and experienced a lot in life. From your vantage point of wisdom and age, what guidance do you have for me?"

She soothed me with her words. "My daughter, what can I tell you? Life is a journey.

"When I married Elimelech, I thought that life could not get any sweeter. He was a decent, good man. He understood that I was his helpmate, not his servant. What an unusual concept for him to adopt, don't you think? He complimented me on my cooking and even helped bring in the firewood. I knew that I was truly a blessed woman.

"When my son was born, I was ecstatic. Because he was small at birth and did not readily take to my breast, I named him Mahlon. However, he soon filled out and became very round. He loved for me to hide my face behind my apron and then peek out at him. He laughed and laughed. Shortly after he was weaned, I discovered that I was again with child. Such an easy pregnancy and birth. Chilion, however, developed congestion in his little chest that never seemed to go away.

"When the famine came, Elimelech tried everything he could to keep us fed so the children would be healthy. Eventually, though, there was no work to be found. Even if we'd had money, there was no food to buy. We could not grow anything because there was no rain. Chilion's cough got worse and worse. The boys grew taller even while we watched both of them begin to have that hollow look. They did not laugh much. They did not tease me with their pranks. They began to withdraw into themselves.

"My husband and I looked at each other one evening while Chilion coughed and coughed. When we crawled under our blankets that evening, we whispered about leaving our home. Elimelech had heard the elders at the gate talking about the abundant food in Moab. That night we decided we would begin packing the next morning in order to take our family to that distant land. We could see no other options for our sons.

"The journey was hard, but we kept our spirits up by talking about all the wonderful foods we would eat when we reached our destination. We finally arrived in Moab. We survived.

"Elimelech and I never really felt as if we fit in. We never abandoned our belief in the God of Israel. We tried to instill the faith of our homeland into our sons, but they did not want to follow our 'old ways.' Mahlon and Chilion made friends with the other young people of the village and learned the Moabite ways.

"Then Elimelech died. He had lived his years. He was simply worn out from taking care of his family. A better husband I could never have had. Even though I always felt that he would die before me, I grieved his death deeply. My sons gathered around and comforted me.

"The boys tried to fill the hole that their father had left in our family. When the time came for them to choose wives, of course, they chose Moabite women.

"My daughters-in-law, Orpah and Ruth, waited on me as if I were a queen. They made sure I was comfortable and well cared for. They rubbed my forehead with unguents to relieve the pain that I sometime had. They brushed my hair, all the while singing songs they had learned as children. Since the songs were Moabite, I did not always appreciate the words, but I loved the way their voices moved with the melodies. I loved Orpah and Ruth because my sons loved them. Both of the young women were good wives and dedicated daughters-in-law. I was truly blessed.

"Our little family began to laugh again, but our laughter was short-lived. A terrible illness swept through our village. Both Mahlon and Chilion died. By this time, I had been in Moab about ten years. I was overwhelmed with grief over my sons' deaths in addition to Elimelech's. I cried enough tears to fill the Sea of Galilee. I could not be consoled. I called myself "Mara," which means "bitter." It seemed that every time I thought that my life was truly blessed, tragedy hit. I was a happy mother and wife when the famine took away my home. I moved to a new land where food was available and believed that once again I was blessed. Then I buried my husband. My sons brought me wonderful daughters-in-law and I looked forward to grandchildren. Before that could happen, I had to bury both my sons. I grieved them, and I grieved the grandsons and granddaughters that I would never have.

"I looked around me. I saw the concern on the faces of Orpah and Ruth.

They wondered what would become of us all. We had no husbands or sons to provide for us. I knew there was no reason for me to stay in this strange land where I did not belong. I had learned from the gossip at the well that the famine was over in Judah. I decided that I would return to Bethlehem, to my relatives, with the hope that one of them would take me in.

"But what about Orpah and Ruth? I did the only thing I knew to do. I told them to return to their own relatives, to their mothers' homes, to marry once again and be happy. I gave them my blessing so they could have full and rich lives. I told them that I wished for them to put the past behind them and to move on to their futures.

"Orpah listened to me. She pronounced her love for me while she drenched my neck with her tears. I smoothed her face, kissed her, and sent her to her future.

"Ruth, however, would not leave. She begged to go with me. She wanted to worship my God and stay with me. What could I do? I could not deny her devotion to either me or my God, so we returned to Bethlehem together.

"Remember I said that life is a journey? As I look back at all the times when I was unhappy or when tragedy struck, I realize that I did not stay in those miserable situations. Things always turned around. The famine in Judah led to life in Moab. Even though I lost my husband and sons there, if we had not moved to Moab, Ruth would never have come into my life. When she and I returned to Bethlehem, I arranged for her to meet Boaz, my kinsman, who took her for his wife. They had a wonderful son, Obed, who was the grandson I thought I would never have.

"My guidance for you is to keep traveling. Stay on the path. Even when you believe that you cannot put another foot in front of you, keep on. I was in the depths of despair. Remember Mara? But now—now—I am Grandmother. There is laughter in my home. Stay committed to being alive. Do not lie down, cry, hide, and refuse to live your life. Believe that the depths will give way to heights.

"The Lord is good. *Never, never* forget that. The journey may not be easy. But the destination is full of blessings. Now go, my child. You've got packing to do!"

"Oh, thank you for your comfort, Grandmother Naomi. You give me hope and blessings from your presence. I'm so glad that you visited." I felt her arms around me again, and then she was gone.

Naomi's Call to Action

- Keep traveling. Stay on the path. Even when you believe that you cannot put another foot in front of you, keep on.

- Stay committed to being alive. Do not lay down, cry, hide, and refuse to live your life.

- Believe that the depths will give way to heights.

- The Lord is good. *Never, never* forget that.

Your Response to Naomi's Presence

1. Do any of Naomi's calls challenge you in your own life or community? If so, how?

2. Does her journey stir up a story for you? If so, what?

3. What did you learn from listening to Naomi?

4. Does her story inspire you to action? If so, what? When? How? Why?

Porch Breezes

> The Lord is my shepherd, I shall not want.
> He makes me lie down in green pastures; he leads me beside still waters;
> he restores my soul. He leads me in right paths for his name's sake.
> Even though I walk through the darkest valley, I fear no evil; for you are with me; your rod and your staff—they comfort me.
> You prepare a table before me in the presence of my enemies; you anoint my head with oil; my cup overflows.

Surely goodness and mercy shall follow me all the days of my life, and I shall dwell in the house of the Lord my whole life long.

—Psalm 23

Awesome God, thank you for the many ways you answer our prayers.

When we pray for miracles, You gently remind us that we already have miracles in our lives, in our family members—old and young.

When we pray for future outcomes, You gracefully remind us that we have today to treasure.

When we pray for strength, You remind us of the prayers that surround us.

When we pray for answers, You bring the unexpected visit, e-mail, card, or phone call.

When we pray for our hurting loved ones, You remind us of others who are devastated with pain or loss beyond our wildest imagination.

When we pray for our loss of normalcy, You remind that many of our neighbors count this kind of distress as normal.

God of Love,

Open our hearts to the fullness of life, with its joys and pains.

Open our minds to the lessons you are providing us as we journey difficult roads.

Open our spirits to the unending joy of living life in You.

Open our mouths to proclaim that You are with us even when we are not sure.

Open our arms to receive the many blessings You continue to send our way.

With hope and love in your grace, we offer this prayer. Amen.[19]

Chapter Fifteen

Ruth—Hope and Expectation

Book of Ruth

Ruth lived in Moab and married Naomi's son. When both women became widows, Ruth chose to return to her mother-in-law's home in Bethlehem. There she married one of Naomi's relatives, Boaz.

When my husband and I started dating, the chemistry between us was immediate. My friends told me that I was disgustingly happy, that I glowed, and that I needed to wipe the ear-to-ear grin off my face. Within days, we each knew in our innermost selves that we wanted to marry, but neither of us said anything to the other. We are both, by nature, shy—Jim more so than I—and had been previously hurt. We both were careful and deliberate in the decisions that we made. So we just enjoyed our time together and kept our secret loves to ourselves. However, by the second month of our dating, we were both assuming that we had a long future together ahead of us.

Jim asked me to marry him after we'd been dating only about ten weeks. We did not tell anyone about our commitment to each other for another month. When our parents learned of our marriage plans, they all were thrilled because they knew that we were primed for happiness.

Our grown children, on the other hand, were, shall I say, less than happy. One of the boys actually said, "Normal people are engaged for at least a year," when he learned that we were planning to have our wedding service in less than four months.

Jim and I were both astounded by how out of character we had acted in deciding to get married. Rather than going over and over in our minds the positives and negatives of our impending wedding, we simply acted on faith, intuition, and strong positive feelings. We acted with belief in goodness and hope for a wonderful life together. We acted out of trust in each other.

As our anniversary approached, I was sitting on the porch, remembering our beautiful backyard wedding. I was feeling blessed in my relationship with this caring and compassionate man. Shortly I realized that I was not alone in my reverie. Another woman was rocking, deep in thought, with her own smile of inner contentment on her face.

I finally broke the spell when I said, "You look like a woman in love."

She smiled and said, "I am. My name is Ruth."

"Hello, Ruth. What words do you have for me from your life journey? How shall I carry on your heritage?"

She answered, "Greetings, sister. I have had a journey indeed. When I was a child, I never dreamed I would have the life I have had. I believed, like all the other women I knew, that I would marry, have children, be a homemaker, and then become a matriarch among my family in Moab.

"I guess the first indication that my life would take a different path was when I married Chilion, an Israelite. My family was displeased that I married an outsider. But he was fair of face and I loved him. We were lovers in every sense of that word. I loved his family as well. His mother, Naomi, was more mother to me than my mother ever was. His brother, Mahlon, and Mahlon's wife, Orpah, extended our family as a committed, compassionate, fun-loving household.

"All that changed when first Mahlon and then Chilion died. The illness that swept through our town took many of the fine, strong, young men. That is when I learned that life has unforeseen changes in it. I discovered to my dismay that I could not lay plans for the future and expect them to turn out the way I dreamed. I learned to live fully in the moment and not in some imagined future that I thought I could control.

"At first, we walked around in a daze. Naomi's husband, Elimelech, had died shortly after they arrived in Moab. Here we were, three widows with no male protector. Orpah and I whispered to each other our guesses of what Naomi might do. We wondered how we would all survive our grief as well as our grumbling stomachs.

"Finally, after the time of intense mourning, Naomi announced that she intended to return to her home in Bethlehem. Orpah and I looked at each other. She told us to return to our mothers' homes, marry again, and be happy. Neither of us had considered this option, so we could not respond immediately to her instructions. We each kissed her, swore our allegiance to her, and walked out of the room. I went to my favorite thinking tree. I do not know where Orpah went. A little while later, we gathered around the table as we prepared our meager meal. We each could see in the other's faces that we were all struggling to make a choice.

"After much indecision, Orpah agreed to stay in Moab and do as Naomi requested. Even so, she wept and held Naomi tight.

"I, on the other hand, could not imagine life without Naomi. She was the loving, caring mother I had always yearned for. She had listened to me from the depths of her being. She had caressed my forehead when I thought I could not possibly cry any more tears after Chilion's death. I was going with her, no matter what she said. She could argue all she wanted with me, but I was determined to go to Bethlehem. I decided that Moab had nothing to offer me. I wanted to live with Naomi and worship her God. I wanted to care for her until the day she died. When I died, I wanted to be buried alongside her.

"There are times when you know you have to abandon everything that is familiar to follow your heart.

"After we reached Bethlehem, I quickly realized that I would have to find a way for us to eat. Naomi had a kinsman, Boaz, who had crops. I asked permission to gather grain from the edge of his field. When I was allowed to glean, I worked without a break from the early morning. I wanted to gather as much as I possibly could for Naomi and me.

"Toward the middle of the afternoon, Boaz himself came into the field. Even though I was hot and sweaty, Boaz must have noticed me. He knew from questioning his laborers that I was Naomi's daughter-in-law. He came to me and told me to continue gleaning in—and only in—his fields. He cautioned me to stay close to the young women who worked for him. He gave me his blessing and offered me food and drink.

"When I told Naomi about these things, I could tell that she was pleased. I could also see that she was beginning to work on a plan.

"As it turned out, Naomi and Boaz worked out the legalities for me to become his wife. We had a precious son, Obed. My great-grandson was none other than King David!

"What I leave with you is the counsel to live with hope and to live expectantly. I would never have believed that my Moabite blood would run through the veins of the greatest king that Israel ever had. I would never have believed that I would find the mother-love I so yearned for. I would never have guessed that I would find not one, but two, wonderful husbands. I never considered that I would leave Moab and find happiness in another country. Every time I thought my life was over, another task came to me that led to the next part of my fulfilling journey. My caring for Chilion led me to Naomi. My desire to care for her led me to Bethlehem. Our need for food led me to Boaz's fields.

"Remember me when you believe that life will always be as bad as it might seem at a particular moment. Naomi's God proved to me that hope is an amazing gift, and that the future is full of gift."

I replied softly, "Amen. Thank you," and Ruth was gone.

Ruth's Call to Action

+ Hope is an amazing gift, and the future is full of gift.

+ There are times when you know you have to abandon everything that is familiar to follow your heart.

+ Live with hope and live expectantly.

+ Remember me when you believe that life will always be as bad as it might seem at a particular moment.

Your Response to Ruth's Presence

1. Do any of Ruth's calls challenge you in your own life or community? If so, how?

2. Does her journey stir up a story for you? If so, what?

3. What did you learn from listening to Ruth?

4. Does her story inspire you to action? If so, what? When? How? Why?

Porch Breezes

O God, you are my God, I seek you, my soul thirsts for you; my flesh faints for you, as in a dry and weary land where there is no water.

> So I have looked upon you in the sanctuary, beholding your power and glory.
> Because your steadfast love is better than life, my lips will praise you.
> So I will bless you as long as I live; I will lift up my hands and call on your name.
> My soul is satisfied as with a rich feast, and my mouth praises you with joyful lips
> when I think of you on my bed, and meditate on you in the watches of the night;
> for you have been my help, and in the shadow of your wings I sing for joy.
> My soul clings to you; your right hand upholds me.
>
> —Psalm 63:1–8

"The especial genius of women I believe to be electrical in movement, intuitive in function, spiritual in tendency."[20]

Chapter Sixteen

Vashti—Claiming One's Power

Esther 1

Vashti was the queen of King Ahasuerus of Susa until he dethroned her after her refusal to come before him and his party guests. He replaced her with Queen Esther. Because of Vashti's disobedience, the king sent a decree that all women, both high and low, would give honor to their husbands.

I went to the porch to try to discern my options for a major decision I was facing. I had learned somewhere in my life that decisions were always right or wrong, good or bad, up or down. When I applied this right-wrong approach to decision making, I got tangled up in emotion, thoughts, and fear. I would feel paralyzed in my process, fearing that whatever I chose would be a bad decision. However, I finally learned that there are almost always additional ways to think about the decisions I was trying to make. I realized with experience the truism, "There is no such thing as a bad decision." A decision might quickly reveal itself to be short-lived, but that information, too, was helpful in making the next decision.

As I was mentally developing options, realistic as well as totally bizarre, about my current situation, Vashti came to see me. I asked, "Who are you?" After she identified herself, I greeted her. "Hello, Your Highness. What path do you have to show me?"

She responded, "There are always options. The king had celebrated for six months with all his officials and ministers, the nobles and governors of the provinces, and the troops of Persia and Media. This gluttonous half-year affair was followed by another week of partying for the men. I gave a party as well for the women. During this frenzied time, the king had displayed all his wealth—linens, silver, marble, and precious and semiprecious stones—and used it in excess everywhere.

"Eventually, the king decided to exhibit me. He ordered me to come into the banquet hall wearing my crown. I have to whisper that he did not mention my wearing anything else. He wanted to parade me around like the servants had paraded all the other *things* he had bragged about. I did not want to do it, and so I refused.

"When a woman refuses to do something a man wants her to do, the man, if he is not worthy in himself, will punish the woman in some way. Many of us women choose to stay with men who ignore us, beat us, and abuse us because we do not want to suffer punishment for our disobedience. Believe me, I know how hard it is to stand up to someone who has that kind of power. Finally, I just knew that whatever was out there had to be better than what I had. I acted on my faint courage and stepped into my future.

"When I made my heroic or stupid stance—it depends on who is evaluating my actions—I inadvertently began a minirevolution in the kingdom. The king was so threatened by my assertiveness that he exploded. He ranted and raved. He knew that everyone in the kingdom would talk about my revolt. That may or may not have been true. There *were* a lot of the dignitaries of the kingdom present at the banquet. The king, my husband, felt he had been bested by a woman. He lost face among his subjects. All the men realized what would happen if their wives claimed their own power and authority. To say that thought frightened the men is an understatement.

"The king did what kings do. He sent a notice throughout the land. He announced that I was no longer his queen and that he would find a replacement for me. He reminded all the men to be masters in their homes, even though he had failed at that!

"My 'punishment'?

"I was not allowed into the king's presence ever again. Ha! I did not want to be in the king's presence in the first place. I got what I wanted.

"When you follow the truth that you know deep inside, you may be scared. You may have to pay a price for your declaration of independence. I demonstrated that you will succeed. I was never again subjected to the king's orders.

"There are always options."

"Your Highness, you give me courage by sharing your story. Thank you." She nodded regally and left me sitting on the porch.

Vashti's Call to Action

+ Follow the truth that you know deep inside. even if you are scared.

+ There are always options.

Response to Vashti's Presence

1. Do any of Vashti's calls challenge you in your own life or community? If so, how?

2. Does her journey stir up a story for you? If so, what?

3. What did you learn from listening to Vashti?

4. Does her story inspire you to action? If so, what? When? How? Why?

Porch Breezes

"When we allow ourselves to exist truly and fully, we *sting* the world with our vision and challenge it with our own ways of being."[21]

"I am not afraid of storms for I am learning how to sail my ship."[22]

Chapter Seventeen
Esther—Acting with Courage and Wisdom

Book of Esther

Esther was the wife of King Ahasuerus. As a Jew and the adopted daughter of her uncle, Mordecai, she was able to prevent an evil plot by Haman to massacre her people.

⟿

One afternoon I went to the porch and deliberately invited Queen Esther to join me. I needed her specific wisdom. All day I had heard in my soul the phrase that her uncle said to her, "Who knows? Perhaps you have come to royal dignity for just such a time as this" (Esther 4:14). Was this where I was as well? Were the opportunities that appeared to be opening for me part of God's divine plan for my life? I did not know. I was not sure. I wanted and needed to speak with Esther.

To my relief and astonishment, she responded to my beckoning and stood on my porch. Knowing that I was in the presence of royalty, I knocked my chair over as I stood up. I knelt before her and said, "Hello, Your Highness. You walked a treacherous path. What can I do to carry on your courage and your heritage?"

She replied, "Please rise and sit in your rocking chair. You do not need to kneel in my presence. I was once a commoner as you are. I am a royal now only because God placed me in my spot in history when Ahasuerus chose me as his bride.

"Let me back up a bit.

"The king, whom I privately called 'Hassi,' decided that he needed a new bride after the disastrous event with Vashti. (You know she refused to come when he summoned her so he could show her off to his friends?) Hassi issued an edict for all the beautiful young virgins in his kingdom to be brought to him so he could choose his next wife. It was a fairy tale. Some of the girls ached to be chosen for this special honor of being brought into the king's harem. Others wept as they were taken away from young men they loved. The last thing most of us wanted was to live for a year in a harem and be used sexually by the king. The ones who were not chosen after their one time with him were doomed (or honored, depending on how one looked at the situation) to live in the second harem as a concubine. For each of us, our beauty and our youth sealed our fate, for good or evil.

"When I arrived at the harem, my Uncle Mordecai, who was my guardian, advised me to keep my Jewish heritage a secret. I could not have articulated why I knew that he gave good counsel; I simply knew that my chances were better if I kept quiet about my lineage.

"I know now that God's hand was at work, but at the time I did not know why Chief Eunuch Hegai took interest in me. He showed me the special tricks that Hassi liked. He taught me the subtleties of makeup and dress that the other girls could only guess at. He provided me with seven maidens to keep me company and to care for me. From the first day I arrived, Hegai treated me as a princess and taught me the hidden rules.

"When you find someone to teach you as Hegai taught me, you are truly blessed. I confirmed with Hegai that he knew how important he was in my life. Whatever I achieved was not only my accomplishment. Hegai, Mordecai, and all people who fasted for me were also part of my ultimate success.

"Because of Hegai's coaching, I was the chosen one. Hassi made me his queen. The coronation party was quite an event, let me tell you!

"I enjoyed the trappings of being royal. What I did not like was all the political intrigue. Uncle Mordecai told me he had discovered an assassination plot to kill Hassi. I relayed the information to my husband and credited Mordecai for my information.

"The next political challenge involved Mordecai and Haman, one of Hassi's officials. Uncle Mordecai refused to bow down to Haman. Mordecai only bowed before the Lord God Almighty and *never* to another person. His refusal infuriated Haman. Haman could not let it go. This one man's slight became to him a huge insult—so huge, in fact, that Haman decided that all of Mordecai's people, the Jews, had to die in addition to Mordecai. Once again a political leader decided to eliminate us. Such is the history of my people.

"Hassi went along with Haman's demand. Did I tell you that my husband was not a very strong man? He went along with whoever was advising him at the moment. Decisiveness was never one of his strong points.

"I remind you that neither Hassi nor Haman knew that I was Jewish. Uncle Mordecai pled with me to come forward to beg for our people. I accused him of not knowing what he was asking of me. Confronting the king about this matter could mean my immediate death. I suggested other options to my uncle but there were none that he could accept.

"Finally Mordecai said these words that changed my heart and gave me courage for what needed to be done. He said, 'Who knows? Perhaps you have come to royal dignity for just such a time as this' (Esther 4:14).

"I planned two successive dinners with Hassi and Haman, never letting on about my background. I used the natural skills that I had. I knew how to delight the king. I had watched Haman and knew how to play to his weaknesses. I fed both men, made them comfortable, skillfully guided the conversation, and then let them wander into the decisions that were the righteous ones.

"During the meal, Hassi remembered that he had never rewarded the one who discovered the assassination plot. That, of course, was my Uncle Mordecai. He asked Haman how to reward someone who had served the king well.

"Haman fell into my plot. He preened, he puffed, and he exalted himself. All this worked in my favor. The reward for Mordecai resulted in the hanging of Haman. Then and only then did I beg for the life of my people and let the king know that I, too, was a Jew.

"Disaster was averted and my uncle and I were richly rewarded. Our people were saved.

"What I have learned is that one's life journey may have twists and turns in it. Who knew I would end up as queen? I believe that each one's path is always under the care of God. Uncle Mordecai was right. I was given royal honors so I could be in the right place at the right time to affect history. I believe that everything that happens in life is preparation for the next step of our God-given journey.

"I also learned that sometimes one can affect history by an indirect route. If I had gone into Hassi's presence and demanded that he reconsider what he was ordering, or if I had confronted Haman about his cruel revenge, or if I had stormed into the court and proclaimed that I was a Jew to be killed along with all the others, then the outcome could have been treacherously different.

"I thought about results I wanted and then considered the best way to go about achieving my goals. As God had led me to the point of the intervention, I trusted that I was being led in the solution. I simply had to stop, think, pray, and ask others for fasting, and then I knew, I *knew*, what my next steps were to be. I did not know what the result would be. I used my best feminine wiles to help my people.

"How can you carry on my heritage? Appreciate your teachers and guides. Remember that you are on a God-given path, no matter what kinds of hills and valleys you encounter along the way. Consider carefully the approach you will take when you have momentous decisions to make.

"You have been an eager subject. I bestow my queenly blessing on you. God speed."

"Dear brave Queen Esther. I will remember your wise counsel. Thank you." I bowed down once more, lowering my eyes in respect. When I looked up, she was gone.

Esther's Call to Action

+ Remember that everything that happens in life is preparation for the next step of our God-given journey. Trust you are being led in the solution.

+ Appreciate your teachers and guides.

- Remember that you are on a God-given path, no matter what kinds of hills and valleys you encounter along the way.

- Consider carefully the approach you will take when you have momentous decisions to make.

Your Response to Esther's Presence

1. Do any of Esther's calls challenge you in your own life or community? If so, how?

2. Does her journey stir up a story for you? If so, what?

3. What did you learn from listening to Esther?

4. Does her story inspire you to action? If so, what? When? How? Why?

Porch Breezes

Our deepest fear is not that we are inadequate. Our deepest fear is that we are powerful beyond measure. It is our light, not our darkness, that most frightens us. We ask ourselves, who am I to be brilliant, gorgeous, talented, and fabulous? Actually, who are you not to be? You are a child of God. Your playing small doesn't serve the world. There is nothing enlightened about shrinking so that other people won't feel insecure around you. We are born to make manifest the Glory of God that is within us. It's not just in some of us, it's in everyone, and as we let our own light shine, we unconsciously give other people permission to do the same. As we are liberated from our own fear, our presence automatically liberates others.[23]

"You don't just luck into things as much as you'd like to think you do. You build step by step, whether it's friendships or opportunities."[24]

Chapter Eighteen

Daughters of Zelophehad—Confronting the Status Quo

Numbers 27:1–11; 36:1–3

Zelophehad—of the tribe of Joseph and father to daughters Mahlah, Noah, Hoglah, Milcah, and Tirzah—died in the wilderness on the journey to the Promised Land. When it came time to divide the new land among the twelve tribes, his daughters—being female and having no brothers—were going to receive nothing. The sisters went to Moses, Eleazar the priest, the leaders, and all the congregation at the tent of meeting and declared that they deserved their father's portion of the land. Moses brought their case before the Lord and the sisters received what they requested.

As part of my responsibilities in a nonprofit organization, I've asked for money from people who believed in our mission or who might be convinced to support our work. At first I was timid. I couldn't imagine that someone would write a check for a thousand dollars simply because I asked them to do it. Of course, that did not happen all the time, but I received positive responses enough times to teach me to be bolder and bolder in my requests. I also finally realized that people would not give if no one asked them to get involved. Much fund-raising literature mentions that the primary reason people do not give is because no one asks them to.

Even knowing all that and with all the experience I had in obtaining the resources we needed, I was facing a daunting challenge. I was planning to speak with a prospective donor who easily could write one check that would cover the budget for an entire year. I certainly was not going to ask for that much money, but the amount I was planning to ask for was significant.

I was also intimidated by the prospect. He had position, power, status, and prestige. Even thinking about speaking with him face to face in his office made my heart pound and my hands sweat. The "ask" meeting was scheduled for the next day. I went to the porch for strength.

It must have been obvious that I needed a lot of reinforcement for this meeting, because five—*five*—women appeared. I was intimidated by so many arriving at once. I asked who they were. One said, "Mahlah Zelophehad." Another said, "Noah Zelophehad." The next one introduced herself as "Hoglah Zelophehad." The fourth said, "Milcah Zelophehad," and the fifth, "Tirzah Zelophehad."

"Hello, ladies: Mahlah, Noah, Hoglah, Milcah, and Tirzah. You are truly amazing women. What call do you offer to me?"

Mahlah spoke first. "I'm Mahlah, the eldest, and so I will speak. When Moses and the other leaders began dividing the land among all the tribes and their clans, we realized that we were going to be left as beggars, without protectors or home. As daughters, we were not eligible to receive a portion of the land.

"We discussed our fate among ourselves. We talked deep into the darkness, night after night. We talked while we did our chores. (Milcah nodded her head vigorously.) Sometimes we ranted in anger. Sometimes we cried. Sometimes we spoke boldly among ourselves. Other times we could only tremble with fear about what was going to happen to us.

"We went over and over what our options were. At first we saw only one: accept the current practice and figure out how to survive. We knew that meant we would have nothing to offer as a dowry. We would have to settle for whoever wanted each of us as wife. Noah especially was concerned, since a fat, old, smelly man of the tribe of Judah was drooling over her anytime we happened to be near him. We definitely wanted land to offer for a decent marriage dowry so we could be honored and happy.

"We assumed we would be separated. That thought was intolerable, since we had survived the wilderness together and knew that we needed each other to manage our new lives in the new land. We also wanted to honor our father by making sure that his name was listed in the official rolls of the new land. If we did not receive an apportionment, he and his part of the family would be lost forever in the memories of our people.

"With all these clear reasons before us, we began thinking about ways we could get our rightful portion. We came up with many elaborate plans. Some I'm even embarrassed to tell you, since they involved unrighteous activities. We would talk about each plan with all its positives and negatives. Then one afternoon while we were baking the bread, Hoglah said, 'Why don't we simply ask them for our share?'

"We looked at each other in silence. Our eyes grew large. What an idea! That was not complicated at all. We would simply march into the tent of meeting and tell Moses what we desired.

"Slowly, ever so slowly, smiles began to break on our faces. Tirzah giggled and I laughed right out loud.

"We realized we needed a strategy for our request. We worked out our approach among ourselves. When we presented our case to Moses, he said that he would have to take it before the Lord. He did and the Lord said, 'Yes!'

"The challenge we offer is to *never, never* accept the status quo. We learned that other options are available as long as you keep looking for them. We simply could have sighed and accepted the rules as they existed. However, we learned that rules can be modified. We also realized that we lost nothing by asking. Moses and the Lord could have said no and we would have been without land. But we were already without land! However, if Moses and the leaders said yes, then we would receive our reward.

"We urge you to think about what you want and be bold in your asking. How can someone say yes if you do not ask?"

"What positive role models you each are. Thank you for visiting me when I needed your advice and courage. You all are awesome." They grinned at me, waved good-bye, and left.

Zelophehad's Daughters' Call to Action

+   *Never, never* accept the status quo.

• Think about what you want and be bold in your asking.

Your Response to the Sisters' Presence

1. Do any of the sisters' calls challenge you in your own life or community? If so, how?

2. Does their journey stir up a story for you? If so, what?

3. What did you learn from listening to the sisters?

4. Does the sisters' story inspire you to action? If so, what? When? How? Why?

Porch Breezes

Everyone who has ever occupied a position in life to which tradition ... opinion ... and habit of mind attribute a certain rigid pattern of behavior, knows very well the ponderous and incessant pressure of public opinion seeking to force one into the mold. Such types as the statesman, the headmaster, the parson, the poet are continually subject to this pressure to become what the public expect them to be rather than what they really are. That very expectation becomes the archenemy, the Satan of the soul. If it is not resisted, the living person becomes a stylized status; he is dead.... This is murder—murder of the spirit—and the murderers are the victim's admirers and friends.[25]

"To know what you prefer instead of humbly saying Amen to what the world tells you you ought to prefer, is to have kept your soul alive."[26]

"I should be uninterested in the fact as to who rules. I should expect rulers to rule according to my wish, otherwise I cease to help them to rule me."[27]

Part Two 🌿

Women from the New Testament

Chapter Nineteen

Elizabeth—Claiming Your Dream

Luke 1

Elizabeth was the mother of John the Baptist, wife of Zechariah, and cousin of Mary, the mother of Jesus.

—❦—

As I was sitting on the porch after work one day, I was thinking about all the ways I had settled in my lifetime. I had settled for a first marriage before I knew my own worth; I had settled for financial security rather than for the risks of new career paths; I had settled for friendships that seemed to require more of me than I received in return.

I was realizing that I no longer wanted to settle. I wanted to live my life as fully as I possibly could. I knew, deep in my soul, that God had more in store for me than I had been willing to claim. There was something in me that was aching for expression, but I was not even sure what that was. The more I considered my past life, the faster I rocked.

The skin on my face glistened with beads of sweat on that humid summer evening as I rocked with more and more agitation. As before, I realized that someone was synchronized with my rocking. I slowed our pace. She identified herself as Elizabeth.

I said, "Hello, Elizabeth. You comforted and sustained Mary in her situation, which was for her both humiliating and exhilarating. You provided her with a woman's love during a time when she needed that special kind of love. You were faithful throughout. I walk with your lineage and your name coursing through my spirit. What wisdom, guidance, and challenge do you have to offer me?"

And this is what she said:

"Oh, my dear daughter in the faith, my namesake. I have loved you as a mother from before you were born. My precious one, I whispered to you in the night when you were a child. I called you by our name—Elizabeth. I murmured words of love and challenge to you. I cooed to you, 'Believe in miracles. Love the Holy One with your whole being. Guide and support those who come to you. God is gracious.'

"I was old when I was blessed with pregnancy. Remember, my child, that blessings and miracles are not only for the young. I repeat what I whispered to you those many nights ago, 'Believe in miracles!'

"Let me tell you a bit about my life before I got pregnant. Zechariah and I had a decent life. He was a respected priest in the temple. There was joy in our lives because we kept God's law. I cannot say that I was totally happy because, as you know, I could not bear a child. A time or two when I thought I was with child, my heart soared. I'd start dreaming of the tiny clothes I'd make and the special songs I'd teach. And then, then ... I would not be pregnant.

"I was a disgrace in my community. Even though I was married to a well-respected man, I was seen as a failure because I could not give him children. My wonderful husband did not have the full status he so richly deserved because he had no heir.

"I had finally gotten to the point where I had reconciled myself to my inadequacies. I was past the age of childbearing. I contented myself with caring for others who needed mothering. Zechariah would let me know of some special need in our community so I could reach out to the person or family, trying to show God's love and care for them. I honestly thought this was to be my special calling—to help expand Zechariah's ministry of righteousness and shalom. I truly enjoyed my involvement.

"Now, however, looking back to that time, I realize that I did not feel fully alive. I did not have the energy, delight, and sublime joy that came into my life through my baby, John.

"I tell you all this so you will continue living with hope and belief in miracles. Do not settle for a substitute life—as important and vital as it may be. Just as I did loving, compassionate, and caring deeds, you, too, may positively affect people and help improve their lives. I ask, 'Are these loving deeds, as important as they are, completely filling you with deep, deep joy? Do you feel connected to the Source of all love and vitality?'

"My child, walk toward your miracle. Run toward what is aching to be birthed in you. Claim your own vital creation to offer to the world. The journey, however arduous it may be, is worth every step.

"Remember, I am your mother in the faith. You are precious. Please come and visit me whenever you need my solace, my care, my nurture, my companionship. I love you, my child, and cannot wait to meet my offspring—in whatever form your insight and creativity takes."

I grabbed her hand with tears in my eyes. I do not know how long I held on to her. She sat with me until I could see her face clearly as my crying stopped. Then she put her hand on my cheek, smiled her blessing at me, and left.

Elizabeth's Call to Action

- Continue living with hope and belief in miracles.

- Do not settle for a substitute life—as important and vital as it may be.

- Ask, "Are loving deeds, as important as they are, completely filling me with deep, deep joy? Do I feel connected to the Source of all love and vitality?"

- Walk toward your miracle.

- Run toward what is aching to be birthed in you.

- Claim your own vital creation to offer to the world.

- The journey, however arduous it may be, is worth every step.

Your Response to Elizabeth's Presence

1. Do any of Elizabeth's calls challenge you in your own life or community? If so, how?

2. Does her journey stir up a story for you? If so, what?

3. What did you learn from listening to Elizabeth?

4. Does her story inspire you to action? If so, what? When? How? Why?

Porch Breezes

I had a profound and very real conversation with Jesus. The clear message I got was that I was learning my lessons that I needed to learn, I was on the path, and when the door was to open, when I was prepared for the door to open, it would—by the grace of God. I was pulled to the story of Jesus' temptation in the wilderness. As the story goes in Mark, Jesus was tempted to turn stones into bread (to break his fast), to jump from a rooftop to prove God's supernatural power, and to have all the kingdoms bow down to him simply by his worshiping the tempter. In Luke, the order is different. I studied some commentaries and other's thoughts on the story. I finally got to the point of what I needed to hear. All the things that Jesus was tempted to do, he finally did in the natural evolution of his ministry. He did indeed feed people (not just himself). He said that he was the Bread of Life. He did demonstrate the miracle power of God in his healings. He did become/was the Lord of the world through his life, passion, crucifixion, and resurrection. He did not renounce forever the things he was tempted to do. He simply renounced the 'how' of those things occurring. I know that the doors will open naturally for me as I live with awareness, lack of fear, and knowledge that the Holy One is opening the door for me in the *kairos* way of time. All I have to do is be open, follow

my intuition, be creative, believe in miracles, and be true to
my inner wisdom.[28]

Trust in the Lord with all your heart,
and do not rely on your own insight.
In all your ways acknowledge him,
and he will make straight your paths.
Do not be wise in your own eyes;
fear the Lord, and turn away from evil.
It will be a healing for your flesh
and a refreshment for your body.
Honor the Lord with your substance
and with the first fruits of all your produce;
then your barns will be filled with plenty,
and your vats will be bursting with wine.
My child, do not despise the Lord's discipline
or be weary of his reproof,
for the Lord reproves the one he loves,
as a father the son in whom he delights.

—Proverbs 3:5–12

Chapter Twenty
Mary—Pondering and Heeding God's Call

Luke 1–2; John 2:1–12; Mark 3:31–35; John 19:25–27; Acts 1:14

Mary was the mother of Jesus, the wife of Joseph. She followed her son in his ministry. Mary has been honored throughout the generations.

⁓

An opportunity was unfolding that might be a catalyst for other doors opening in my professional life. But I was also uncertain if I was capable of the new expectations. I wanted the chance *and* I was timid about the next steps. I went to the porch to sit with the possibilities that were imminent. The air was cool that day. I was lazily rocking, feeling the slight breeze on my bare legs, when I was joined by a woman. As I looked to see her face, I noticed an inner glow that drew me in comforting ways. I waited for her to speak. She finally said, softly, "I am Mary."

"Hello, Mother Mary. You were chosen by God to be the mother of God's son. You have walked a path of both joy and pain. What do you have to give me, your daughter in the faith?"

She replied, "My sweet daughter, you honor me. I'll speak to you as a woman and not as a saint—which is how some people treat me. They want to put me on a pedestal with a heart and emotions as cold as the stone from which my statue is carved. I am flesh and blood, through and through, with the feelings of a woman and a mother. I speak to you as Mary, wife of a carpenter, Joseph, and mother of the man, Jesus.

"I was betrothed to Joseph but before we 'lived together,' I became pregnant.

"A messenger from God, an angel, told me that I had been chosen to bear the Son of the Most High. The angel's first words were, 'Greetings, favored one! The Lord is with you' (Luke 1:28). I was astounded. The way the angel spoke, it sounded as if I had already been blessed—certainly through no effort on my part. I was a peasant, with neither wealth nor fame.

"Then the angel admonished me, 'Do not be afraid, Mary, for you have found favor with God' (Luke 1:30). The angel continued by telling me that I was going to get pregnant and that this was *a very special baby*.

"Do you know what my first comment was? 'How can this be, since I am a virgin?' (Luke 1:34). Can you believe that I questioned the *logistics* rather than the *significance* of the pronouncement?

"Then the angel told me that nothing is impossible with God. So I, with a big gulp and my eyes wide and a little glazed over, replied, 'Here am I, the servant of the Lord; let it be with me according to your word.' (Luke 1:38).

"The impossible had just been announced. From depths that I did not know I had, I found strength and my center. This is what I hope for you. There may be times when you are asked to handle the impossible, when you think that the task is beyond you, and when you know that there is absolutely no way that you can do what is being asked. I just knew that someone else had more credentials, more wisdom, and more experience for bearing God's son than I did. I pray that when God comes calling, you too will find inner focus and will walk with God on the path that is before you. God will enable you to be bigger than you can imagine for yourself!

"Now let me tell you, that path may not be simple. The words I spoke to the angel were easy in comparison to the life tasks for which I had been chosen. I watched my son die on a cross, for God's and humanity's sake.

"I felt I had no choice but to take God at God's word. Just think about it. I was betrothed. In a lot of ways, I was a newlywed. I left my parents and Joseph and stayed three months with my older cousin, Elizabeth, whom God also led to become pregnant. Outrageous? Yes! Here I was at a time in my life when I needed and wanted to be with the man I would spend the rest of my married life with, a time when I really needed my mother's help to get through the early days of pregnancy, and I went off to Elizabeth's in the hill country.

"When I arrived, Elizabeth immediately *knew* about me and my baby boy, Jesus. Outrageous? Yes! But being with Elizabeth was exactly where I needed to be at that time, and somehow I knew that.

"I was very blessed during my stay with my cousin. I encourage you to find someone who can confirm your call to you, someone who can nurture you in those early, tentative explorations of the journey you are on. Elizabeth knew how to teach me what I needed for that particular time. She shared with me from her wisdom and life experience. She listened to me, for hours on end, as I went over and over my conversation with the angel. She told me the old story of Hannah, who also offered her son, Samuel, to God, as I would have to do. She sang to me Hannah's song of praise to our God.

"Name and then go to your own Elizabeth.

"For nine months, I had a lot to ponder. I had no more clue about my future than any other mother has about the future when discovering that she is pregnant. 'Why was I chosen for this responsibility? Do I believe that I have been honored or punished? What does it mean to be the mother of the Son of the Most High? What is going to happen between Joseph and me? How in the world do you train someone to become the heir to the throne of David? What is God asking me to do? Why is God asking me to do this? Is there any way to say no to God?'

"And then later, when Joseph and I were traveling to Bethlehem, I meditated on what I was going to do if the baby came while we were on the journey. The thought crossed my mind that giving birth to the Son of the Most High might mean the circumstances for the birth would be vastly different than what they turned out to be. Having the Son of God in a barn? Outrageous! I confess that at times I wondered if I had had some fantastic dream and that my understanding of the specialness of my baby was only a figment of my imagination.

"When the shepherds came and told me about their own special visitation from the angel, I began believing more strongly that I and my son would have special roles in the future. I trembled when I got the merest glimpse that we might affect the history of the world. I began to be scared for my child. I felt overwhelmed with the immensity of the job that God had given me.

"So what did I do? I treasured all the words of the shepherds and pondered them in my heart.

"I learned that when you have an interaction with the Holy God, you are stopped in your everyday life by a divine connection. My angel was named Gabriel. Your angel may be a sudden insight that surprises you by its wisdom and clarity. It may be a change of heart about someone or something that did not come from inside you. You may have a conversation with someone who says just the exact words you need at that time. Your angel may be an itch to follow a yearning, to do something outrageous, or to step out of your usual ways of being. You may become aware that a strength of yours has become a weakness in certain arenas, and that a weakness is now a strength. You may have a dream that seems to speak to you from other realms of the universe. You may have visions or powerful knowings that you believe come from God. The angel Gabriel may even visit you!

"I believe that you have to ponder these kinds of visitations to discern God's guidance. How would I have ever known about the magnificence of the shepherds' visit if I had not pondered the event over and over?

"Pondering is holy activity. And yet, how often do you ponder the things of your life? You worry, you stress, you ignore—but do you really ponder? Pondering is considering the events with calmness, a way of looking at an event from several different angles, knowing that each angle is both accurate and inadequate. Pondering contains a sense of knowing and yet not knowing. There is almost a sense of 'This is what I know now and I'm open to knowing even more—today, tomorrow, during my life.'

"When I stopped to think about God's activities in my life, I have to admit that I was somewhat afraid of what I would find. I was scared that God would ask me to change who I was, what I did, and how I lived my life. That was a very legitimate fear. Look what happened to me! You, too, may be afraid that your carefully designed world of work, home, friends, and family may be totally disrupted.

"And yet, I can honestly say that I would not have had it any other way. I would not have given up my encounter with God and its results even if I had known at the time what I learned later. Maybe what happened to me *was* risky, but what an outcome! And certainly the impact of the intervention by God continued to make itself real as I pondered the past, the present, and the future.

"Pondering is well worth it. Time spent thinking about how God has interacted in my life and continues to do so is the most wonderful gift that I can give myself, and one you can give to yourself. Pondering is a treasure that we can receive from God.

"So, my child, seek your Elizabeth, ponder God's interaction in your life, and above all, with God's help, be bigger than you ever thought possible."

I was so overwhelmed by Mary and her words of comfort and call that I could only close my eyes in gratitude to God for this wonderful gift. When I opened them again with praise and wonder, I realized that Mary had left the porch—but I did not feel alone.

Mary's Call to Action

- I pray that when God comes calling, you too will find inner focus and will walk with God on the path that is before you. God will enable you to be bigger than you can imagine for yourself.

- I encourage you to find someone who can confirm your call to you, someone who can nurture you in those early, tentative explorations of the journey you are on.

- Name and then go to your own Elizabeth.

- Ponder God's interaction in your life.

- With God's help, be bigger than you ever thought possible.

Your Response to Mary's Presence

1. Do any of Mary's calls challenge you in your own life or community? If so, how?

2. Does her journey stir up a story for you? If so, what?

3. What did you learn from listening to Mary?

4. Does her story inspire you to action? If so, what? When? How? Why?

Porch Breezes

> And Mary said, "My soul magnifies the Lord, and my spirit rejoices in God my Savior, for he has looked with favor on the lowliness of his servant. Surely, from now on all generations will call me blessed; for the Mighty One has done great things for me, and holy is his name. His mercy is for those who fear him from generation to generation. He has shown strength with his arm; he has scattered the proud in the thoughts of their hearts. He has brought down the powerful from their thrones, and lifted up the lowly; he has filled the hungry with good things, and sent the rich away empty. He has helped his servant Israel, in remembrance of his mercy, according to the promise he made to our ancestors, to Abraham and to his descendants forever."

—Luke 1:46–55

God-chosen girl:
What did you know of God
    that brought you to this stable
    blessed among women?[29]

Chapter Twenty-One

Anna—Knowing and Praising

Luke 2:36–38

Anna was in the temple in Jerusalem when Jesus' parents brought him to be consecrated. As a prophet, the widow of Phanuel of the tribe of Asher, she immediately recognized that the baby in Mary's arms was the redeemer of her people.

Whenever my friend and I get together, we share the tales of our lives since we last saw each other. We talk about family members—both the aggravating things they've said or done as well as the funny things. One member of my family is especially hilarious to her. And this is the embarrassing part. When my friend laughs, she laughs with her whole body. She shakes, tears stream down her face, her mouth flies open, and she screams—she screams with wave after wave of mirth. And of course, when she laughs like that, I have to laugh too. I have been accused of having a less-than-ladylike laugh as well. We thoroughly enjoy ourselves while everyone sitting around us glares at us for disturbing their bland, quiet lunch. We are disruptive to the staid ambience of the restaurant. People glance to see what we must have been drinking with our meal (iced tea or water, always!).

I was reminiscing about the lunch we'd had that day, when we'd once again gotten "those looks." I sat on the porch, thinking about all the experiences, good and bad, that she and I had shared through the years. I had a small smile on my face and my eyes were closed as I was seeing her in my mind's eye—laughing like a crazy woman. When I opened my eyes, an older woman who identified herself as Anna was there. She was giggling as she rocked. Her eyes twinkled with energy.

I watched her face wrinkle with overflowing joy for a moment before I said, "Hello, Mistress Anna. From your vantage point of age, wisdom, and insight, what words do you have to offer me?"

She paused for only a moment before speaking.

"Do you believe in holy timing? I certainly do. The fact that I was in the temple when that poor couple came in was God-timed. Even though I spent a lot of hours worshiping and praying in the temple, any number of things could have kept me from being so blessed. I arrived at the temple later than usual that day because I had spilled milk on my clean floor just as I was leaving my home. Of course, I had to wipe it up before I could leave. Praise the Lord.

"Be aware of those holy synchronisms. Never take them for granted. Be grateful for those times when you are detained. There is a reason that your timing was altered. God knows better than you. You may never know why things happened like they did. Just think. That spilled milk meant that I was at exactly the right place at the right time. Praise the Lord.

"The baby in the swaddling clothes was just another baby in the eyes of many of the pilgrims in the temple. The family was one of many families who were dedicating their firstborn sons to the Holy God. I, because of the gift of prophecy that the Lord God had given to me, could recognize the truth of Simeon's words when he proclaimed, 'My eyes have seen your salvation, which you have prepared in the presence of all peoples, a light for revelation to the Gentiles and for glory to your people Israel' (Luke 2:30–32). When you see something or someone who deserves your praise, be generous with it. And because I knew Simeon spoke truthfully, I wanted to shout to everyone, 'Praise the Lord!'

"I knew … I knew … that this tiny child was the Messiah of the world. How did I know, you ask?

"Well, in part I knew because I heard Simeon singing. Simeon's song rang true to me because of God's gift of special insight. But there was more. Sometimes you simply *know*. You do not know how you know. You just *know*. Learn to trust that knowing, that insight, that intuition. As you grow into that gift, you will learn what is of God and what is not. What is of God will be proven to be true. I knew, without any doubt, that the baby was the Savior of the World. Certainly that has been affirmed. People who followed after me have confessed Jesus as the Christ. You have proclaimed that truth as well, I believe. Praise the Lord.

"I started praising God and telling everyone about the one I had seen. I sang of the goodness of God in sending the Messiah during my lifetime. I did not encounter anyone to whom I did not announce my good news. Many thought me a crazy old woman. They thought I had finally slipped into the confusion of my age. Praise the Lord.

"I did not care. So what if people thought me crazy? I had seen the light of salvation. I had touched his sweet face. I had seen the love of his parents for him. What more could I do? The dream that I did not dare to dream had been fulfilled. An old woman had been granted the opportunity to see the greatest gift that our God had ever given to us! Of course I ran around acting crazy. I am certainly not the first person to be so filled with love and joy for God that people raise their eyebrows. Praise the Lord.

"Let go of your 'proper' behavior when you are filled with exultation. Sing and shout as if no one were around you. Share your joy with everyone. Folks can use some excitement in their otherwise bland lives. Be alive with the Spirit. That's what the world needs—your energy, your aliveness, and your proclamation of the good news.

"You asked for my words of wisdom: Trust holy timing. Be generous with your praise. Let people think you are crazy!"

At that, I laughed and laughed until tears ran down my cheeks. What a wonderful freeing feeling. "Thank you, Anna." She danced from the porch.

Anna's Call to Action

+ Be aware of those holy synchronisms. Never take them for granted. Be grateful for those times when you are detained. Trust holy timing.

+ When you see something or someone who deserves your praise, be generous with it.

+ Learn to trust that knowing, that insight, that intuition. As you grow into that gift, you will learn what is of God and what is not.

+ Let go of your 'proper' behavior when you are filled with exultation. Sing and shout as if no one were around you. Share your joy with everyone.

+ Be alive with the Spirit. That's what the world needs—your energy, your aliveness, your proclamation of the good news.

+ Let people think you are crazy!

Your Response to Anna's Presence

1. Do any of Anna's calls challenge you in your own life or community? If so, how?

2. Does Anna's journey stir up a story for you? If so, what?

3. What did you learn from listening to Anna?

4. Does Anna's story inspire you to action? If so, what? When? How? Why?

Porch Breezes

Deliver me, O Lord, from evildoers; protect me from those who are violent,
who plan evil things in their minds and stir up wars continually.
They make their tongue sharp as a snake's, and under their lips is the venom of vipers.
Guard me, O Lord, from the hands of the wicked; protect me from the violent who have planned my downfall.

The arrogant have hidden a trap for me, and with cords
they have spread a net, along the road they have set snares
for me.

I say to the Lord, "You are my God; give ear, O Lord, to the
voice of my supplications."

O Lord, my Lord, my strong deliverer, you have covered my
head in the day of battle.

Do not grant, O Lord, the desires of the wicked; do not
further their evil plot.

Those who surround me lift up their heads; let the mischief
of their lips overwhelm them!

Let burning coals fall on them! Let them be flung into pits,
no more to rise!

Do not let the slanderer be established in the land; let evil
speedily hunt down the violent!

I know that the Lord maintains the cause of the needy, and
executes justice for the poor.

Surely the righteous shall give thanks to your name; the
upright shall live in your presence.

—Psalm 140

"If you surrender completely to the moments as they pass,
you live more richly those moments."[30]

Chapter Twenty-Two
Mary of Magdala—Being Blessed and Truth-Telling

Luke 8:1–3, 24:11–13; Matthew 28; Mark 16; John 20:11–18

Mary of Magdala was healed of demons by Jesus. She became one of his followers. She is the first person who saw the risen Christ.

Frank was a seminary buddy. He'd had a hard life and was one of those people to whom certain church folks loved to listen. Frank's story was one of boy-gone-bad, horrible decisions and life choices made, prices paid, and conversion later in life. All this led to Frank becoming an evangelist for the gospel of Jesus Christ. His personal testimony meant that he was a popular speaker, especially for adolescent groups and youth retreats. Nevertheless, he was an outsider in the seminary family, as was I.

There was only a handful of women students in the student body. Not only that, I was extremely and vocally opinionated in those days, and still had many rough spots to deal with if I was going to survive in the church in the South as a minister.

Frank and I connected, two outsiders who loved seminary and felt deeply called to be ministers in our own ways.

The summer after graduation, I still did not have a call to minister. Frank came to see me one day. I was despondent because no one seemed to want to claim my gifts for service in the church. I whined and whined.

I blamed all kinds of things for my continuing lack of the call that was a prerequisite for ordination to Minister of Word and Sacrament in the Presbyterian Church, USA.

Finally Frank had had enough of my self-pity and complaints. He said, "You may never be ordained to ministry in an official capacity in your denomination. However, you will be God-ordained by anyone who chooses you to minister to him or her, in whatever way that comes."

I was mulling over that long-ago conversation one day when I felt more like a bureaucrat than an ordained minister. I tried to remember people who were not in my denomination who had indeed claimed me as their minister. They shared deep pain or exultant joy; they sought my guidance; or they asked for prayer or blessing. As I sat on the porch, hoping that the holy space would soothe my soul, I began to be filled with a sense of someone being with me, someone who knew in her deep heart some of what I was experiencing. I asked her name.

"I am Mary of Magdala, sometimes called Mary Magdalene."

"Hello, Blessed Mary. Please tell me what you want for me to carry on as your legacy."

I'll share with you what she shared with me.

"When my beloved Jesus was preaching on the mountain, one of the many thrilling and challenging things he said was, 'Blessed are you when people revile you and persecute you and utter all kinds of evil against you falsely on my account. Rejoice and be glad, for your reward is great in heaven, for in the same way they persecuted the prophets who were before you' (Matthew 5:11–12).

"I believe this is what happened to me. I have been reviled and persecuted—not directly and openly, but with innuendo and silence. I am comforted that Jesus calls me blessed because of that.

"Jesus cured me of seven demons that inhabited me. I do not want to try to describe to you what my life was like during that dark period. Suffice it to say that I would *never* wish for anyone to have to endure the agony and suffering I went through during that time in my life.

"Jesus is the person who gave me back my reason to live. I gave him my life, followed him everywhere, and listened to everything he said. I soaked up his kindness, his insights, and his love of God. Whatever small things

I could do to lighten his burden, I did. I mended his robe after he snagged it on a mustard tree. I brought him bread and wine when he finally took a break from teaching the crowds that followed him everywhere. I helped the children get close enough to be able to see him.

"Jesus was able to be himself when he was around me. He could complain about the sun beating down on his head or about how his feet hurt from a day's long walk. He explained to me more in depth about the things he taught the crowds.

"Occasionally some of his other disciples got a little jealous, I think, about the special connection I had with Jesus. They appreciated how I was able to care for him and make his life a little easier, *and* they resented the time I spent with him.

"After Jesus' agonizing death on the cross, many of the men hid from fear. I, however, along with some of the other women, was determined to anoint his broken body. I knew that we could do this last small thing for the man who had loved each of us so much.

"What we discovered when we went to the tomb was so shocking and wondrous that different versions of what happened were developed. It all depended on who was telling the story as to what the exact details were.

"Matthew said that Jesus appeared to me and the other Mary and told us to tell the disciples to meet him in Galilee. Mark depicts a man in white inside the tomb giving those same instructions to Mary (James' mother), Salome, and me. Luke said that two men in dazzlingly clothes told me, Joanna, Mary (James' mother), and the other women that Jesus had risen from the dead. According to Luke, the men did not believe us until Peter had seen for himself the linen grave cloths lying in the tomb.

"John's version is, of course, the one that I know to have happened. Jesus appeared to me alone in the garden. I ran to the other disciples saying, 'I have seen the Lord' (John 20:18).

"I do not think that they believed me until they saw Jesus for themselves, later that day.

"As the days and weeks continued and we struggled without leadership, our little band began to move into its next stage. We wanted, no, we were compelled by something greater than ourselves to tell what we had experienced and what we knew. Peter and James, the brother of Jesus, each had convincing reasons for why he should be considered our leader. They argued, they quoted Jesus, and they looked to our traditions as Jewish people. At times, when the discussions got too fierce, someone would look at me and say, 'Mary, you often had conversations with Jesus. What do you think he would say?' After I had given my interpretation, the argument would cease ... for a while.

"I began to notice that every time someone in the group deferred to my opinion, Peter and James would sit up taller, press their lips together in a tight, straight line, and narrow their eyes. It seemed that they did not want to hear what I, a woman and confidante of our Lord, had to say. I began to sense that I was slowly and carefully being eased out of the inner circle. My opinion was no longer being solicited. My voice was deliberately and systematically being silenced.

"And then I began hearing rumors. It seems that when Martha's sister, Mary, washed and anointed Jesus' feet, others began whispering about the perfume she used. They began to insinuate that the oils she used were the ones that prostitutes used. No one ever accused her of being a prostitute. After all, she was Lazarus' and Martha's sister. But when Matthew wrote of an unnamed woman anointing Jesus' head, also in Bethany, people began, in earnest, to say that a prostitute had anointed Jesus with her professional oil. It was not too long before the rumors said that that woman was me and that I was a prostitute. With this falsehood, I was officially discredited.

"From that moment on, I was effectively silenced by the group and later by the Christian church that grew from our work.

"I moved to a small home in the area near Magdala and spoke with whomever visited me about Jesus the Christ and who he was in my life. I told stories of my journeys with Jesus so they could know Jesus as I knew him.

"'Blessed are you when people revile you and persecute you and utter all kinds of evil against you falsely on my account.' Sometimes we do all we can, we are true to what we know, we know that Jesus still deeply loves us, and—we may be silenced even so.

"When you can stand up to that silencing, by all means do so. When you notice that other voices are being silenced, do what you can to make sure they continue to be heard. When none of that works as you wish it would, remember you are blessed. Jesus said so! What more do you need?"

"Dear Mary, what a wonderful witness you are to the power of Jesus's love in your life. Thank you for your presence." We rocked a bit longer. Finally I realized that I was once again alone.

Mary of Magdala's Calls to Action

- When you can stand up to silencing, by all means do so.

- When you notice that other voices are being silenced, do what you can to make sure they continue to be heard.

- When none of that works as you wish it would, remember you are blessed.

Your Response to Mary's Presence

1. Do any of Mary's calls challenge you in your own life or community? If so, how?

2. Does her journey stir up a story for you? If so, what?

3. What did you learn from listening to Mary?

4. Does her story inspire you to action? If so, what? When? How? Why?

Porch Breezes

"God does not necessarily select the noblest or most deserving person to carry out Divine purposes."[31]

Listen to Me

When I ask you to listen to me and you start giving me advice, you have not done what I asked.

When I ask you to listen to me and you begin to tell me why I shouldn't feel that way, you are trampling on my feelings.

When I ask you to listen to me and you feel you have to do something to solve my problems, you have failed me, strange as that may seem ...

When you do something for me that I can and need to do
for myself; you contribute to my fear and weakness.

But when you accept as a simple fact that I do feel what
I feel, no matter how irrational, then I can quit
trying to convince you and get about the business of
understanding what's behind this irrational feeling.

And when that's clear, the answers are obvious and I won't
need advice ...[32]

Chapter Twenty-Three
Woman Who Hemorrhaged—Choices

Matthew 9:20–22; Mark 5:25–34; Luke 8:43–48

For twelve years a woman bled. When she reached out and touched the bottom of Jesus' robe, she was healed.

My friend Jo developed breast cancer, and by the time she was diagnosed, she had stage four metastatic disease. When she visited me, we would sit on the porch and cry together. Some days she would be confident that she would beat the illness. Other days, she felt that death was imminent. Still other times, we did not even talk about her illness but talked about the kinds of things we always talked about.

Jo is a healer. Her primary mode of offering relief to others is through massage therapy, healing touch, and energy work. As word of her cancer got out in her small community, she noticed that some of her clients no longer wanted to come to her, even though, most days, she was physically able to work and indeed needed to work for her emotional and financial health. She began hearing that people were afraid to come to her because she had cancer. They did not want to get the disease themselves.

The day she sat on my porch, crying from fear that she might lose her house due to inability to make her mortgage payments, we realized that we had been joined. Jo looked at me with surprise, since she did not know about the women who talked with me on the screen porch. Jo looked back and forth, and said, "I knew that this porch was a special place, but wow! I never expected this! Who are you?"

The woman replied, "I have no name, but for twelve years, I bled. I am now healed."

I jumped in. "Hello, healthy woman. Because of this experience of healing, you have insights to share that can guide us on our way. Please talk with us."

And she did.

"I am nobody. You do not even know my name. And yet you choose to listen to me. I do indeed have something I would like to share with you. But my gleanings have nothing to do with me and everything to do with him, Jesus.

"For twelve years I hemorrhaged, which meant I was horribly unclean. I was totally alone—absolutely shut off from the worship of God and from the fellowship of other men and women. The bed I slept in was unclean, the chair I sat in was unclean. Any item I handled was unclean, so that if anyone touched that same item, that person became unclean as well. Leviticus states that, 'Whoever touches these things shall be unclean, and shall wash his clothes, and bathe in water, and be unclean until the evening' (Leviticus 15:27).

"Please do not ever do this to anyone—ostracize someone because of an illness. The disease itself is bad enough. To also have to live with the loneliness, the strong sense of unworthiness, and the utter desolation is much worse than the actual illness.

"It's not that I did not try to get well. I did. I tried everything. I spent all my resources on doctors, to no avail. Not only did they not heal me, my condition actually became worse. I once had money and position but now was an outcast. My money and my former prestige had not protected me from this terrible illness.

"I tried all the medical options I had available. There was no cure. My life was literally seeping out of my body. Finally I reached out in desperation to an alternative way of healing, although I did not know it at the time. In touching Jesus' hem, I reached for the healing of my spirit as well as my body.

"When I touched Jesus, I was made well. I did not simply stop bleeding. I was made well, whole, complete. I was given, in that touch, my love of life and my knowledge of my purpose in life. No medical doctor using traditional methods had been able to do that! Only someone with holy, healing energy could make me well through and through. Jesus, the Son of God, felt my presence and healed me in miraculous ways through his spirit, his energy, his love, and his compassion. He did not even have to touch me with his hands! His healing love gave me back my life.

"In reaching out to Jesus, I felt that I was reaching out one last time before my life ended. I knew that I had nothing more to lose. I should not have been in the crowd. Every person I touched, even inadvertently, became unclean. My life was filled with humiliation and isolation. I took tremendous risks that day in a final attempt to turn around my life. My actions were indeed very bold. I was in a public place, with no male protector, and I dared to touch a strange man. How could I have been more scandalous?

"I'm not sure whether I was that desperate or that full of faith.

"I reached out slowly and with fear, but also with courage and deliberation, to touch the tassels on Jesus' garment. And immediately I was healed. It was like a light going through me. Then Jesus exclaimed, 'Who touched me?' (Luke 8:45). The focus of the crowd at large suddenly zoomed in on Jesus and me—a close-up in the most real sense of the word.

"What had I done? I had made this holy man unclean. I, who had been ostracized from all of society, was now suddenly the center of attention. I was no longer sick, but was I yet whole? Was I still defined by my unclean condition?

"I fell on my knees and confessed what I had done and why I had done it. I did not know what the consequences of my behavior might be from either Jesus or the crowd.

"And then Jesus truly healed me through and through when he said, 'Daughter, your faith has made you well; go in peace' (Luke 8:48). I, who had had no family or protector, was now called 'Daughter.' Jesus gave me his blessing. Through the encounter, I regained my health—physical, emotional, and spiritual. I reclaimed my position in society as well as a new outlook on life. 'Go in peace,' he said.

"Now that I was healed, I had tremendous decisions to make. These I share with you for whatever help they may be for you.

"After I was healed, I realized that I had become accustomed to being sick. I knew what being an outcast felt like. I knew, after twelve years, how to be alone. Now, all of a sudden, my illness no longer defined me. I had no excuse for being disengaged with life. I no longer could avoid taking responsibility for all the chores of my life. Before my encounter with Jesus, I could say, 'I cannot do that because whatever I touch will become unclean.' Now those reasons were no longer valid.

"I had a new challenge in my life—to live as a healthy, whole woman. The previous twelve years could have continued to limit me in terms of how I perceived the world and my relationships in it. I could have let my history continue to write the script for my present and my future. I could have continued to be an invalid, about to die at any moment. God knows I had envisioned my death numerous times.

"Now, with Jesus naming me 'Daughter,' placing me back within the human family, calling me back from the brink of death, I had a choice. Did I want to live as a person of life—or of death?

"If and when you are faced with a new definition of yourself, I hope that you too will smile and call yourself 'Daughter' and be part of the human family in the most alive way you know to be.

"Jesus gave me this wonderful gift. All I could do was honor it by living completely and thoroughly with the time I had left. I hope that you will be willing to reach out and touch the hem of Jesus' garment, and then live with the results."

Jo, for once in her life, was speechless. As she looked with gratitude to this woman and then to me, she deeply relaxed and we were alone … but together.

Healed Woman's Call to Action

- You have a choice. Do you want to live as a person of life—or of death?

+ When you are faced with a new definition of yourself, smile and call yourself 'Daughter,' and be part of the human family in the most alive way you know to be.

+ Be willing to reach out and touch the hem of Jesus' garment, and then live with the results.

Your Response to Healed Woman's Presence

1. Do any of the healed woman's calls challenge you in your own life or community? If so, how?

2. Does her journey stir up a story for you? If so, what?

3. What did you learn from listening to the healed woman?

4. Does her story inspire you to action? If so, what? When? How? Why?

Porch Breezes

At the time of this writing, Jo's cancer has metastasized to her bones. She is choosing to live life as fully as she possibly can.

> "Hope is not what we find in evidence, it's what we become in action."[33]

> "[Jim] Wallis' test of social work is: Will what you are doing change your life?"[34]

Chapter Twenty-Four

Syro-Phoenician Mother—Calling for What Is Right

Matthew 15:21–28; Mark 7:24–30

A Syro-Phoenician (Canaanite) woman confronted Jesus about healing her daughter from the demon that tormented her. When Jesus did not respond as she wanted him to, she kept insisting that he help her. He did as she requested.

My sons were not perfect, I'll be the first to admit. But let someone else try to put them down, demean them, hobble them from becoming the men God was creating them to be, and I moved into action. No one, not one person on the face of this earth, not a relative, not a teacher, not a friend, could go after my sons inappropriately. I would protect them in whatever way I could. That might mean challenging a false label being placed on them by someone who supposedly had their best interests at heart, or calmly hearing complaints about them, after which I dealt with my sons as necessary. I tried to focus on ways of addressing their behavior that certainly got their attention and yet also affirmed their humanity. I must admit that sometimes I too fell into the mire of devaluing their spirits when I acted out of my own frustration and sense of limitations.

I noticed that the same feelings would sometimes get stirred up in me when I was working for others whom I believed were being denied the basic services they needed to live full and complete lives. When I was at my best,

I was their staunchest advocate. When I was not operating from my highest motives, I was sometimes seen as attacking, and knew that I inadvertently ended up with the opposite result from what I was working for.

I was rocking on the porch trying to calm myself. I had spent the morning arguing with a governmental agency that was procrastinating in providing services for someone I was helping. I had not handled the confrontation well. The person I was trying to help was, I'll admit, difficult, but that did not mean the agency employee had to be mean and nasty. I had fed into the negativity of the situation and instead of adding calm, I added heat. I was on the porch going over and over the conversation in my head—what I should have said, what I wished I'd said, and what needed to be said.

As I was fuming, the chair beside me began rocking. By now, I'd come to expect that someone would appear when I needed sustenance. She was rocking faster than I was, but soon we coordinated our backward and forward motions. Since I was in a nasty mood, I snapped, without graciousness, "Who are you?"

She responded, "You call me the Syro-Phoenician woman, the one who challenged Jesus to heal my daughter."

"Hello, Mother. I remember you. You fought like a mother bear. What is your legacy for me?"

She reminded me of her story.

"You are right. Where my daughter was concerned, I became as aggressive as I could to protect her. When I asked Rabbi Jesus to help me, he reminded me that he came only for his people, the Israelites. I was Canaanite and should not have bothered him. But bother him I did.

"I have gotten ahead of myself.

"For more than half of her life, my daughter had talked to people who were not in the room. She rocked back and forth for hours and hours at a time. She seemed to hear things that I could not hear. I had taken her to all our local healers, but they could not help her. I tried doing all the things that the priestesses of our gods suggested. I made sacrifices during each holy day. My poor daughter continued her speeches to the air.

"I was desperate. I wanted, no, I needed her to be healed. Her form was so beautiful and her spirit was so ugly. I yearned for her spirit to match her physical appearance. I wanted her to return to the time when she could stay clean and keep her hair combed and bound.

"My nephew, Daniel, worked for a cloth merchant. The master whom he served often sent him into Israel to deliver orders to customers. While there, Daniel occasionally heard of a teacher who was attracting large crowds. His name was Jesus. He healed people, taught them, and showed compassion for the crowds. The man they called Jesus always made sure they had food to eat. He taught about his God by telling stories.

"One day, between deliveries, Daniel was standing at the edge of a crowd gathered around this teacher. A woman stood beside Daniel, watching and listening to this Jesus. She murmured her praises of the teacher. Daniel did not quite hear her and asked her to repeat what she had said. She told him she had lived among the tombs because she was inhabited by seven demons. Jesus had healed her, and now she was one of his followers.

"When Daniel returned home, he came to my house, both for my date cakes that he loved to eat and to tell me about this healer. As he spoke, my heart began to pound. I got light-headed and had to sit down. From that moment on, I knew I would travel to find this man so he could heal my daughter.

"Before I was able to finalize my plans to go to Israel, I heard when I was at the well that a man named Jesus was in our region. All my friends were twittering about the things he was doing and saying. I knew this had to be the one Daniel had seen.

"I practically ran home, spilling water along the way. I left my jar at the threshold and went out in search of Jesus. Finally I heard murmuring and followed the sound. As soon as I got near enough to see him, I began screaming at him (see Matthew 15:22). I needed to speak loudly to get his attention. I needed him to acknowledge me. I begged him to heal my daughter.

"His reply astounded me. He did not sound like the compassionate healer that I had heard about. He said, 'Let the children be fed first, for it is not fair to take the children's food and throw it to the dogs' (Mark 7:27).

"That should have been the end of the conversation. But it was not.

"This is where I believe my legacy may apply to you. I did not accept his answer. Can you believe that? I was a foreigner to him. He did not know me at all. I was *demanding* that he do something!

"I knew that this rabbi was not doing right for my daughter. When I challenged him, he gave me an answer that made sense to him and should have silenced me. He basically told me that he was only for the lost sheep of the house of Israel (Mark 15:24). But I knew, I *knew*, that he was not correct. I knew there were other options, other ways to look at the situation.

"Now, I could have meekly accepted his reply and slunk away fuming. Or I could do what I did, essentially saying, 'No. That is not right.'

"I know there are many ways to speak truth. I could have been pleasant and reasonable. I could have said, 'That may be true. However, I see it this way.' I could have made faces of incredulity that anyone would even think such a thing, much less say it.

On this occasion, I chose to use Jesus' own words in response to his statement. I pointed out that even the dogs eat crumbs that fall from their master's table.

"And do you know what?

"When I said that, Jesus told me my faith was great (see Matthew 15:23) and my daughter was healed!

"When you begin to work for what you believe is righteous, I caution that you may be sidetracked as I almost was. When Jesus began talking about dogs, I could have reacted to my perception that Jesus had called me a dog. No matter that he used the term for a household pet. I still did not like being put in that category.

"The God of Israel must have been with me, a woman of Syro-Phoenicia, because I ignored the implication and stayed focused on my true agenda—getting my daughter healed. And praise the Israelite God, my daughter was clear-headed when I returned home. She was once again beautiful in spirit as well as countenance, and remains so to this day.

"The moment I walked into my house and saw my daughter, I knew, I *knew* that Jesus was holy. The Canaanite gods were not powerful. Only the God of Jesus' stories was the one true God. I knew that I could petition this God and the Holy One would hear me. I did not need to fear in approaching Jesus' God with matters of righteousness.

"Remember all I have told you. Have courage and strong faith. Now go out and call for the healing of the world, with God's help."

"Yes, ma'am. Thank you for this speech, which gives me a strong backbone. You are an exquisite example of fighting for someone you love or for something you believe in. I applaud you." She thanked me for allowing her to spend time with me and share her story. Then she left.

Syro-Phoenician Mother's Call to Action

+   When you begin to work for what you believe is righteous, I caution you that you may be sidetracked as I almost was.

+   Stay focused on your true agenda.

+   Remember all I have told you. Have courage and strong faith.

+   Now go out and call for the healing of the world, with God's help.

Your Response to the Syro-Phoenician Mother's Presence

1.   Do any of the mother's charges challenge you in your own life or community? If so, how?

2.   Does her journey stir up a story for you? If so, what?

3.   What did you learn from listening to the Syro-Phoenician mother?

4.   Does her story inspire you to action? If so, what? When? How? Why?

Porch Breezes

"Forces that threaten to negate life must be challenged by courage, which is the power of life to affirm itself in spite of life's ambiguities. This requires the exercise of a creative will that enables us to hew out a stone of hope from a mountain of despair."[35]

To you, O Lord, I call; my rock, do not refuse to hear me, for if you are silent to me, I shall be like those who go down to the Pit.

Hear the voice of my supplication, as I cry to you for help, as I lift up my hands toward your most holy sanctuary....

Blessed be the Lord, for he has heard the sound of my pleadings.

The Lord is my strength and my shield; in him my heart trusts; so I am helped, and my heart exults, and with my song I give thanks to him.

—Psalm 28:1–2, 6–8

Chapter Twenty-Five
Woman Who Was Bent—Joining Jesus in Healing

Luke 13:10–17

This woman was bent over for eighteen years until one Sabbath when Jesus healed her. Immediately she stood up straight and praised God. The leaders in the synagogue were not happy that Jesus healed her ... on the Sabbath. Jesus helped them understand their shameful stance concerning her improved health.

Just as I was about to get into my car to slip out of the office early, Tiffany appeared from behind a bush and called my name. "Ms. Beth, Ms. Beth. Can I talk with you?"

I've known Tiffany for years. She has fought addiction, sexual and physical abuse, and victimization for most of her life. Most of the time she loses the battle. She occasionally experiences victory for a time. On this day, she was highly agitated and distraught. She was crying, cursing, and physically demonstrative with her anger. I knew not to get too close to her, and she, to her credit, acknowledged that she would stand several feet away from me.

I asked her what was going on. She said, "They say I'm paranoid, that I see things. Of course I see things. I live on the streets. I *have* to see things. I have to pay attention to what is going on around me. If I don't, I'm dead. They say I'm crazy. I'm not crazy. *I'm not crazy!*"

I asked a few more questions, trying to understand what was currently going on. I found out she was staying in a homeless shelter. This situation was an improvement, because the last time I'd spoken with Tiffany, she was living under a bridge. However, things were not going well at the shelter. Other residents were out to "get" her. I also learned that she had been approved to move into an apartment that could be hers for the rest of her life as long as she was not a danger to herself or others. To be eligible for this wondrous opportunity, she had to meet three qualifications. She had to be seriously mentally ill, she had to have a drug problem, and she had to meet the federal definition of homelessness.

I asked Tiffany if she truly wanted to move into the new place. She emphatically said, "Yes."

"Well, then, you have to have a diagnosis of mental illness. I don't know if you are crazy or not, but the diagnosis is required for you to be eligible."

We went over pieces of the conversation several more times. She apologized for her language and calmed down enough to say, "I don't want to sabotage this. I know this is God's gift to me. I have to think about the higher goal." Then she asked me to pray with her. Within two weeks, she moved into a beautiful one-bedroom apartment that is all hers, complete with a key!

While I was rocking on the porch and enjoying the scent of the magnolia tree that was in full bloom, I was glowing in the joy of this interaction with Tiffany and filled with gratitude for the possibility of true hope for her. I was joined on this day by a woman who sat very straight and tall in the chair beside me. She smiled at me encouragingly.

So I spoke. "Hello. Who are you?"

She replied, "I am the woman who was once bent over but now, as you can see, I am very sturdy and erect."

As I had learned to do, I asked, "What do you call me to do to honor you and continue your legacy?"

She replied with dignity, "Jesus healed me of the demon that had bent my body for eighteen long years so that I could not stand up straight. When I was upright, all I could think to do was praise God. What else *could* I do? I was hurt when the others challenged Jesus for helping me! I understood their position because the Sabbath-keeping laws were very strict. I hoped they would overlook the rules since a miracle had happened! For just a moment, I was afraid that Jesus might listen to them and put that old spirit right back into my body so that I'd be looking at the ground for the rest of my days.

"There are many people like me—bent over. Oh, they might not look like I did. They might be crippled with all kinds of afflictions: demons, abuse, or poverty. They might be bent over because they have spent all their time meeting others' needs and did not or could not care for themselves.

"I ask you to see these people in your midst. As Jesus healed me, be part of his healing touch for all those others who are crippled by life. Jesus gave me a life that I had never dreamed possible, one I could only have hoped for. Will you be Jesus' hands and heart for someone like me?

"I was extremely grateful that Jesus was not bound by the attitude, 'This is the way we have always done it!' Jesus did what needed to be done—*period*! He set me free from bondage. He did not consider the personal cost to him because of the criticism he would receive. He simply had compassion on me and stood me up straight.

"When Jesus reached out to me, he knew that he could lose friends or some of his well-earned reputation. I am relieved that he did not ask, 'Why try?' believing that he could not do anything. He knew that he took a risk in healing me. I acknowledge all this.

"Knowing the risks, I still ask you to remember me. See me standing tall and straight with my hands in the air, with my feet spread far apart, with a smile as big as the crescent moon, shouting 'Glory to God in the highest.' See me singing, 'Praise the Lord! Praise the Lord, O my soul! I will praise the Lord as long as I live; I will sing praises to my God all my life long' (Psalm 146:1–2). Think of me caring for my family. See me sharing the burdens of other people in my community who are still bent over. See me praying and praising God. See me swirling and dancing and running and leaping. See me whole.

"Then can you follow Jesus' example? I pray so."

All I could say was, "Let's dance and praise God." And we did until she left.

Tall Woman's Call to Action

- I ask you to see bent-over people in your midst.

- As Jesus healed me, be part of his healing touch for all those others who are crippled by life.

- Be Jesus' hands and heart for someone like me.

- See me whole.

- Then can you follow Jesus' example? I pray so.

Your Response to the Tall Woman's Presence

1. Do any of the woman's charges challenge you in your own life or community? If so, how?

2. Does her journey stir up a story for you? If so, what?

3. What did you learn from listening to the tall woman?

4. Does her story inspire you to action? If so, what? When? How? Why?

Porch Breezes

More than 925 million people (one in seven) know what it's like to go to bed hungry every night.[36]

There is no county in our country where someone earning minimum wage can afford a two-bedroom apartment at fair market rent.[37]

The United States places last among nineteen countries when it comes to deaths that could have been prevented by access to timely and effective health care.[38]

Chapter Twenty-Six
Woman at the Well—Crossing Artificial Boundaries

John 4:3–32, 39–42

A Samaritan woman happened to be at the well at midday when Jesus stopped by and asked for a drink of water. Even though it was forbidden, she conversed with him about theology and her situation. Afterward, she returned to the city, telling everyone to come and see this man who she thought might be the Messiah.

Who am I to speak? I've traveled little. I have suffered the pain of divorce. I have lived in the same city for most of my life. I have no doctoral degrees. I simply do what needs to be done. I listen to the small voice that resides in my heart. I am not connected with anyone who is famous. I don't even know how to program my technology gadgets. Who am I to preach, teach, or write?

These questions made me gasp for breath in anxiety as I rocked on the porch one evening. I could see the lightning bugs, hear the tree frogs, and occasionally hear a car's engine rev up on a nearby street. But these normal sounds did not soothe my tormented soul in the warm darkness. I lit a candle as the darkness became thicker.

Who am I to think I have something to say? Who am I?

Even in the dim light, I noticed the chair beside me begin to rock. A face appeared in the candlelight, a face that glowed with both delight and amazement. I looked at her quizzically.

"I am the woman at the well," she said.

"Hello, Mistress. From your encounter with Jesus, you certainly have some wisdom to share with me. What can I do to carry on your encounter with the Christ?"

She said, "It is only because of Jesus the Christ that you want to talk with me. Prior to his changing my life, you would have avoided me and probably even looked down on me. I know this because of the rejection I experienced over and over before my life-changing conversation with Jesus.

"The other women drew their water when the heat was not as intense as it was at midday. But if I came when they were gathered at the well, I had to endure their cold shoulders or, worse, their petty comments. Some of them felt sorry for me, but most of them looked down on me.

"That fateful—shall I say faithful?—day, I saw someone already at the well as I drew near. I braced myself for insults. And then I realized that it was even worse. There was a man at the well. I'd gotten in trouble before for speaking to a man who was not my husband. I wondered what this man would do.

"As I came closer I was horrified to discover that this man was a Jew. Jews hated us Samaritans. They called us half-breeds. They said we were unclean and that we worshiped foreign gods. Jews hated us, and there was one sitting at the well.

"I thought about what I could do. I could turn around and go home without water. That was not an option, since the consequences of having no water would be disastrous. Finally, I decided to draw my water and pretend that he did not exist and that I was invisible. I hoped that I could fill my jar and nothing would happen.

"One thing I would ask you, if you think you can do it, is to reach out to people like me—people who are outsiders, people who are invisible to your kind of people, and people who are not 'good' as you define good. What happened next showed me that when people who care reach out to those of us who feel that no one does, amazing things happen.

"I noticed that the man looked tired. When he asked me for a drink, I only stared at him in wonder. I retorted, 'How is that you, a Jew, ask a drink of me, a woman of Samaria?' (John 4:9).

"He was not supposed to speak to a woman except one who was his wife or his daughter, and he certainly should not have considered drinking from my cup. I'm Samaritan *and* a woman—even more despised. He would become ritually unclean if I honored his request. But I could tell that he was thirsty and the sun was hot. What could I do? If I did not honor his request, I feared that he might collapse from thirst and the heat, and then what would I do?

"He chatted as I dipped water for him. He began talking about someone giving me living water—spring water. Not smelly cistern water or deep-to-draw well water, but fresh, bubbling water. Glorious water, cool, clear spring water. Living water!

"Then I knew that the heat had gotten to him, because he had no bucket and the well was deep. I felt he was making fun of me. Who did this Jew think he was? Did he think he was better than our patriarch, Jacob, who had given us this well? Was he insulting my ancestor?

"Then he said, 'Everyone who drinks of this water will be thirsty again, but those who drink of the water that I will give them will never be thirsty. The water that I will give will become in them a spring of water gushing up to eternal life' (John 4:13–14).

"What a gift he offered to me. To never be thirsty again ... to never have to come in the heat of the day to draw water ... to never have to subject myself to the ridicule of the other women ... to be relieved of this burdensome task!

"Then the man moved deeper into my life. No longer was he talking about the tasks I did each day when he talked about living water. Now he began talking about my personal situation. He said, 'Go, call your husband, and come back' (John 4:16).

"At first I misunderstood. I wondered why I needed a man to draw water, since drawing water was woman's work. What did a husband have to do with anything, especially since I had no husband now? I had only the kindhearted man who took me in after I had been cast off yet one more time. He did not want to see me forced to live in sin, so he and his family took me in. He was very compassionate to provide for me, especially since he was not my relative.

"This man at the well, this Jesus, moved right to the most painful place in my life. I had had five husbands. Some people thought I was immoral. And I guess, by some ways of thinking, I was. But I truly had tried everything to give sons to each of my husbands—to no avail. Each man put me aside for a variety of reasons: burning dinner, speaking with a man, walking with my head uncovered, or, sorrow of sorrows, not having children—especially sons. The prophet Malachi condemned all women like me when he said, 'And what does the one God desire? Godly offspring' (Malachi 2:15). But does being barren really make me immoral?

"No matter. This Jew knew that I had been married five times. I did not detect any judgment on his part. He referred to my husbands as a matter of fact. He did not look down on me. He did not turn away from me. He did not condemn me. And yet he knew me. He knew the pain I had in having had five husbands. He knew how I felt, knowing that I was powerless. He knew what I was—unwanted. Still he talked with me. He engaged me.

"Because Jesus *knew* me, I realized that he was more special than I originally saw. I said to him, 'Sir, I see that you are a prophet' (John 4:19). From there, the conversation moved to styles of worship. Then he told me he was the Messiah.

"Before I could say anything or absorb what he had said, other people came up. They appeared to know him. I could see them bristle when they saw us talking. So I left my water jar and hurried away.

"As I was walking back to the city, I started thinking about what Jesus had said. He said that he was the Messiah. A Jewish Messiah. Yeah. That sat well with us Samaritans. But he *did* know all about me.

"He dealt with my curiosity about his lack of a water jar. He had knowledge that was impossible for a traveler through Samaria to know. I decided I would ask someone when I got to town—that is, if anyone would talk with me. They might brush me aside as being crazy from the heat. They might shun me once again. They might laugh at me.

"I knew that if Jesus really was the Messiah, everyone would want to see him and talk with him. I just did not know. I argued with myself. Should I risk rejection one more time? He *did* talk with me. *He* risked that. *His* people were astonished with him for talking with me. Couldn't I take a risk and tell others about *him?* He broke all the rules to speak to me. I wanted some help in thinking about him. Could he be the Messiah?

"Then I decided. I announced, 'People, listen! Come and see a man who told me everything I have ever done. Yes, he told me everything. What do you think? Can he be the Messiah? Come and see for yourself. He said that I have had five husbands and that the one I have now is not my husband. Everything! He knows me. Come with me. Hurry. He might leave before you see him. Hurry. He might be the Messiah. He's at the well. Hurry.'

"And do you know what happened next? The people listened. They invited the man—this Jesus—to stay. And he did. Imagine a Jew staying for a couple of days as a guest of Samaritans—sleeping in our beds, eating our foods out of our utensils, talking with us, and teaching us. Nothing like this had ever happened to us.

"My neighbors then gave me the ultimate compliment. They said, 'It is no longer because of what you said that we believe, for we have heard for ourselves, and we know that this is truly the Savior of the world' (John 4:42).

"They had listened to me! My faith was not complete, but they listened. The Savior of the world used me to spread his message—a woman with no power and five husbands, a woman whom nobody would talk *to* but only talk *about.* Jesus used me to introduce him to Samaria.

"Now my neighbors talk about me as the one who led them to the Savior. I am no longer the woman no one wants.

"Now, I'll return to your question about sharing my wisdom.

"Be like Jesus was with me. He moved beyond 'being nice.' He talked with me. He was *real* with me. I was hurting and ashamed. He provided me a safe space to share my pain. He engaged me in conversation and listened for the messages under the words. He helped me pull out the damaged parts of myself by looking with compassion, not judgment, at my sores, denials, deceits, and failures. With love and care, he treated my 'confessions' as facts that I could now trade for wholeness, justice, and mercy. He listened to me, the person who was talked about. I was considered invisible, and he led me to a relationship with him. I was hated by the people in my community, and Jesus crossed those artificial boundaries.

"Are there painful places where Jesus can look in your life and touch the pain there? Just as Jesus didn't judge me, he won't judge you. He will focus healing light on your sorrows and wash them with his fresh, bubbling, spring-fed, living water. After Jesus told me all that I had ever done, I could then wonder if he was indeed the Messiah.

"Go with my blessing, carrying the peace of knowing that your Savior knows you and loves you anyway."

"Dear friend, you are an inspiration and quite a witness to our Lord Jesus Christ. Thank you." As she walked away from the porch, I noticed she carried a water jar … just in case.

Samaritan Woman's Call to Action

+ Reach out to people like me—people who are outsiders, people who are invisible to your kind of people, and people who are not "good" as you define good.

+ Be like Jesus was with me.

+ Provide a safe space for people to share their pain.

+ Engage people in conversation and listen for the messages under the words.

+ Help pull out the damaged parts of someone by looking with compassion, not judgment, at sores, denials, deceits, and failures.

+ Cross those artificial boundaries.

+ Go with my blessing, carrying the peace of knowing that your Savior knows you and loves you anyway.

Your Response to the Samaritan Woman's Presence

1. Do any of the woman's calls challenge you in your own life or community? If so, how?

2. Does her journey stir up a story for you? If so, what?

3. What did you learn from listening to the Samaritan woman?

4. Does her story inspire you to action? If so, what? When? How? Why?

Porch Breezes

Six Principles of Nonviolence

1. Nonviolence is a way of life for courageous people.

2. Nonviolence seeks to win friendship and understanding.

3. Nonviolence seeks to defeat injustice not people.

4. Nonviolence holds that suffering can educate and transform.

5. Nonviolence chooses love instead of hate.

6. Nonviolence believes that the universe is on the side of justice.[39]

> Therefore, since we are justified by faith, we have peace with God through our Lord Jesus Christ, through whom we have obtained access to this grace in which we stand; and we boast in our hope of sharing the glory of God. And not only that, but we also boast in our sufferings, knowing that suffering produces endurance, and endurance produces character, and character produces hope, and hope does not disappoint us, because God's love has been poured into our hearts through the Holy Spirit that has been given to us.
>
> —Romans 5:1–5

Chapter Twenty-Seven
Sister Mary—Following Your Heart with Loving Acts

Luke 10:38–42; John 11:1–45; 12:1–8

Mary was Martha's and Lazarus' sister. While Martha is known for her hospitality skills and her assertiveness, Mary was known for sitting at Jesus' feet and listening to him. Later on, she anointed his feet with perfume and dried them with her hair.

My mother's sister, Ned, was eleven years older than she. Aunt Ned was widowed for more than thirty years and never had any children of her own. My brothers and I, along with our cousin, satisfied some of her longing for children of her own. She crocheted doll clothes for me and made me a wonderful stuffed doll that could dance with me when I slipped the elastic bands attached to his shoes to my own feet. Not a birthday passed that I did not get a card from her. She always signed it with "I love you" or "Lovingly, Aunt Ned."

Many, many people received handwritten notes from her. She might include a funny story she found somewhere or an inspirational poem that she either wrote herself or cut from a magazine. As she got older, her eyesight began to fail and her hands could no longer be trusted to write legibly. When Aunt Ned moved into a health-care facility sixty miles away, my mother helped her continue with her correspondence to friends who lived back home. Since her own minister was no longer available, I contacted her former minister who lived in her new town. When I asked him to visit her in the nursing facility, he replied, "Your aunt is very special to me. I continue to receive notes from her. She has the gift of appreciation and affirmation."

The evening after Aunt Ned's funeral, I was sitting on the porch, admiring the potted plant my mother had sent home with me from the mortuary. Sister Mary gently touched my hand and introduced herself as Martha's sister.

"Hello, Sister Mary. What would you have me do to honor your legacy?"

She responded, "Oh my! No one's ever asked that of me before. My sister, Martha, is the one who usually gets asked that kind of information. I'm not sure I have anything to offer that would be helpful to you.

"Martha certainly saw me as household help. She loved me dearly. I do not mean to imply otherwise. It's just that she seemed larger than life to me—so accomplished. I, on the other hand, was only adequate in bread baking and mending. She was in charge in our home, making sure everyone had plenty to eat. She handled all the affairs at Lazarus' death. She watched for Jesus even while overseeing the caring for all the mourners. All I could do was cry and try to do whatever insignificant tasks she gave me.

"When Jesus came to our house, Martha made sure to prepare all his favorite foods: figs, bread dipped in fragrant olive oil, goat cheese, and dates. He knew how much she loved him from the many ways she pleasured his palate.

"What I could do was listen to him—which he seemed to like. I knew I should not be sitting as one of his students, because everyone knew that only males could study with rabbis. But Jesus did not find my presence a problem and even encouraged me in my learning. I sat and soaked up the truth and love in his words. I hardly said anything myself.

"Because I was so meek in his presence, I never knew if Jesus understood how much I loved him. I lay awake at night trying to think of something to give him—something as special as Martha's fig cakes.

"During that last visit—even though we did not know at the time that it was Jesus' last visit—I looked at him with love in my eyes. I tried to absorb all his features: his face, his shoulders, his hands, and his feet. When I looked at his feet, I remembered sitting at those blessed feet while I listened to him talk (even though Martha had asked Jesus to chastise me and send me into the kitchen).

"I peered intently at his road-weary feet and thought, 'I can massage his feet! I can wash the grime off and rub perfume on his cracked skin!' And so I did.

"I used the best, most lavish scented oils I had. I used the oil generously, never thinking of the extravagance of the perfume. Then I unbound my hair to show my devotion to this man. I dried his feet with my hair. From his response of gratitude, I knew deep within my soul that Jesus knew how much I loved him.

"So ... what can you do to carry on my legacy?

"Follow what you know to be important even when you are going against the rules of your culture. I knew that I was *supposed* to help Martha prepare the food and serve all our hungry guests, but I could not bear to be away from Jesus and his teaching. Thank heaven Martha's passion was hospitality. Otherwise we would never have eaten!

"I admit that it is not easy committing yourself to such learning, such devotion as I had.

"People thought I was lazy or a dreamer. Some thought I should have given the money that was spent on the perfume to help others. They wanted me to feel guilty for my act of love and devotion. All those other people did not realize that I was soaking up honey for my soul.

"Pay attention to what your soul is hungry for. Feed it—no matter what or who tries to prevent the nurturing of your God-centeredness.

"Focus on ways to drench people with extravagant love. For some reason, we expect those we love to know that we love them. We do not tell them. We do not do special things just for them. But that expression of love is essential for us both, the lover and the loved.

"I am grateful that I was able to anoint Jesus' feet before his agonizing death. Otherwise, I would have been tormented with wondering if he had known how much I loved him. Because I risked showing him, even to the point of being criticized for my actions, I know that he knew. He *knew* my love for him.

"Tell those you love. Show those you love the depth of your affection, commitment, and devotion to them. You never know when you'll see them for the last time.

"I encourage you to take your love and devotion one step further. Move beyond thinking only about people in your life. Who are others who need you to share with them about Jesus? I ask you to consider how you will demonstrate to Jesus the depth of your love for him. Oh, I know, he already knows what is in your heart. How will *you* show him?

"Whose feet will you anoint? You remember, he said that when we do acts of love and kindness to others, we are doing them to him.

"Ponder how you'll show Jesus how much you love him. *Then do it!*"

"Amen and Amen, gentle sister! Thank you." Then I was alone, left to think about whose feet I needed to wash.

Sister Mary's Call to Action

- Follow what you know to be important even when you are going against the rules of your culture.

- Pay attention to what your soul is hungry for. Feed it—no matter what or who tries to prevent the nurturing of your God-centeredness.

- Focus on ways to drench people with extravagant love.

- Tell those you love. Show them the depth of your affection, commitment, and devotion to them. You never know when you'll see them for the last time.

- Move beyond thinking only about people in your life.

- Consider how you will demonstrate to Jesus the depth of your love for him. How will *you* show him?

- Whose feet will you anoint? You remember, he said that when we do acts of love and kindness to others, we are doing them to him.

- Ponder how you'll show Jesus how much you love him. *Then do it!*

Your Response to Sister Mary's Presence

1. Do any of Mary's charges challenge you in your own life or community? If so, how?

2. Does her journey stir up a story for you? If so, what?

3. What did you learn from listening to Sister Mary?

4. Does her story inspire you to action? If so, what? When? How? Why?

Porch Breezes

"'Lord, when was it that we saw you hungry or thirsty or a stranger or naked or sick or in prison, and did not take care of you?' Then he will answer them, 'Truly I tell you, just as you did not do it to one of the least of these, you did not do it to me'" (Matthew 25:44–45).

"Jesu, Jesu, fill us with your love, show us how to serve the neighbors we have from you."[40]

Chapter Twenty-Eight
Martha—Hospitality and Faithful Living

Luke 10:38–42; John 11:1–45

Martha's home was a place where Jesus found hospitality and comfort. Along with her sister, Mary, and brother, Lazarus, she ministered to Jesus.

⁓⸱

Urgent or important? That's a question I have to make myself stop and consider on occasion. Is what I'm spending my time on urgent or important? The urgent tasks at the office (answer my e-mails, respond to the voice mails, write this memo, set up that meeting, prepare for this presentation, etc.) are often urgent. However, they do not fill my soul. They fill my time, allow me to put a lot of checkmarks on my to-do list as I complete the actions. At home, laundry, cleaning dog hair from the floor yet again, and changing bedsheets are all urgent. The chores need to be done—but they do not fill my soul.

Writing, listening to meditation tapes, spending time with different family members, and connecting with friends are important. These actions nurture my spirit. They require me to postpone or totally ignore the things that are urgent so I can focus on the things that are important.

My sons were in kindergarten and first grade when I began my seminary education. The course assignments, the papers to write, the tests to prepare for, all required much time—more than the day seemed to offer for me. My sons wanted my attention, the house always needed something, and meals needed to be prepared. Much of my life was urgent.

But time with my sons was important. I discovered that if I spent about twenty minutes playing a board game with them, they were satisfied for a time. As an added benefit, they allowed me about forty-five minutes of uninterrupted time to work on a paper. Focusing on what was important assisted me in completing what was urgent in unexpected ways.

One of the important things for me is spending time on the porch. Martha introduced herself and joined me there one afternoon.

"Hello, Mistress Martha. From your vantage point as hostess and follower of Jesus, what challenge do you cast at me?"

This is what she shared with me.

"'Thank you. I am pleased to visit with you. I brought a tin of goodies. Can I offer you a fig cake, perhaps, or a drink of cool water? No? Well, then.

"I was blessed to be able to take care of Jesus, my Messiah, the Son of God. How many people can say that? I cooked food for him. I provided a bed for him to rest on when he stopped by our home, weary from his journey. I provided for him as I did for my own brother and sister. What was mine was his. I was very touched, and, yes, proud that he felt as comfortable as he did in my home.

"I challenge you to create hospitable environments for people who live with or visit you. I know that many people believe that hospitality requires the best in furnishings and decor. Some people think that everything has to be perfect for someone to feel welcomed in their homes. The towels cannot be frayed, the walls need to be freshly washed, and the floors have to be spotless. I confess that I got caught up in being the perfect homemaker and hostess. I finally got it through my head that providing hospitality is *not* about serving fancy meals or having everything look like Herod's palace. Hospitality is about being willing to sit with your guests and truly listen to them. Of course, the food still has to be prepared, but it does not have to be elaborate, just nourishing.

"I realized finally that the greatest compliment someone could give to me was, 'I always feel so welcomed and comfortable in your home. The space feels serene and almost sacred.' When I was buzzing around keeping beverage cups filled, worrying if the table was properly set with linens and dishes, fussing over complicated meals that required constant attention and stirring, and picking up clutter while others were sitting chatting, I was not creating a serene space. I was creating anxiety.

"So be hospitable, not anxious, when you have guests.

"Thank the good Lord that I finally realized I could be a good hostess as well as listen intently to Jesus. I joined my sister Mary as one of the disciples who sat at Jesus' feet. You did not know that? Yes, I was an eager learner. Being around Jesus, one could not help but be engaged with him.

"When Lazarus died and Jesus came, I immediately and easily proclaimed to Jesus that I knew he was the Messiah, the Son of God, the one coming into the world. How did I know this? On one hand, I knew it because of the hours I had spent with him—feeding him, listening to him, and simply being with him. To be in his presence meant that I experienced the Holy God.

"On the other hand, I cannot tell you how I knew, without a doubt, that Jesus was the long-awaited Savior. I guess that God called that confession forth from me just like Jesus called Lazarus from the grave.

"My other challenge to you is to listen for that God-wisdom that is already breathed into you by God. After you have heard that voice, proclaim it.

"Can you imagine? I, a woman, on par with Peter? How is that, you ask?

"Peter declared that Jesus was the Messiah, the Son of the living God. (I did not know this at the time when I spoke to Jesus. I learned it much later.) I also said to Jesus, 'I believe that you are the Messiah, the Son of God, the one coming into the world' (John 11:27). Separately, one man and one woman pronounced statements of faith that have since been known throughout the centuries!

"This insight, an insight which you too have if you but listen for it, meant that I could readily proclaim, 'I believe.'

"Spend time learning from the Master. Read from the Scriptures. Talk with others who are walking in His Way. Listen expectantly for God's voice. Then proclaim to God and everyone, 'I believe.'

"Oh, yes, there's one other thing. I learned that even when you think your world has come to an end, as I did when my brother Lazarus died, you may be wrong. I never, *never* dreamed that Jesus would bring Lazarus back to life. But it happened. You may not have a loved one die and then be raised up, but you can hold on to the reality that with Jesus by your side, new life *will* rise from your grief and despair. You will find new reasons for life to continue and even be joyful after a time. You will experience relationships and connections that you never anticipated. You will be embraced by love when you thought that love would never be in your life again. How those things happen—reasons for living, relationships and connections, love—is beyond my knowledge and explanation. Who can explain what happened to Lazarus?

"I challenge you to claim that death is not the last word, that grief can be lessened, and that you can be totally astounded by God's actions.

"So, be hospitable in a nonanxious way, listen to God's voice and proclaim your faith, and always live knowing that joy is on the way, no matter what.

"Now would you like some of those fig cakes?"

"Thank you, Mistress Martha. The cakes smell wonderful." As I bit into one, she left the porch.

Martha's Call to Action

- ✦ I challenge you to create hospitable environments for people who live with or visit you. Be hospitable, not anxious when you have guests.

- ✦ Listen for that God-wisdom that is already breathed into you by God. After you have heard that voice, then proclaim it.

- ✦ Spend time learning from the Master.

- ✦ Read from the Scriptures.

- ✦ Talk with others who are walking in his Way.

- ✦ Listen expectantly for God's voice.

- Proclaim to God and everyone, "I believe."

- I challenge you to claim that death is not the last word, that grief can be lessened, and that you can be totally astounded by God's actions.

- So, be hospitable in a nonanxious way, listen to God's voice and proclaim your faith, and always live knowing that joy is on the way, no matter what.

Your Response to Martha's Presence

1. Do any of Martha's calls challenge you in your own life or community? If so, how?

2. Does her journey stir up a story for you? If so, what?

3. What did you learn from listening to Martha?

4. Does her story inspire you to action? If so, what? When? How? Why?

Porch Breezes

"How do I love God? ... By doing beautifully the work I have been given to do, by doing simply that which God has entrusted to me, in whatever form it may take."[41]

Above all, maintain constant love for one another, for love covers a multitude of sins. Be hospitable to one another without complaining. Like good stewards of the manifold grace of God, serve one another with whatever gift each of you has received. Whoever speaks must do so as one speaking the very words of God; whoever serves must do so with the strength that God supplies, so that God may be glorified in all things through Jesus Christ. To him belong the glory and the power forever and ever. Amen.

—1 Peter 4:8–11

Chapter Twenty-Nine
Dorcas—Reaching Out with Your God-Given Gifts

Acts 9:36–43

Dorcas cared deeply for widows, making garments for them. They were devastated when she died. And then, miracle of miracles, when Peter came to her deathbed, she was resurrected!

———

I have always known about Dorcas in the Bible. My mother's name is Dorcas, and she used to sew my clothes when I was growing up. When I was in high school, my mother found a dress pattern that she especially enjoyed using. The design was simple and fit me well. She made a number of dresses for me using that particular pattern. Each one looked different because of the trims she added, the accessories she found, or the design in the material she chose. Because sewing was important to her, she decided that I too needed to learn to sew. She sent me to sewing classes at the sewing machine store because for one thing, she needed to get me out of the house that summer, and for another, she knew that I would pay more attention to my teacher than to her.

To this day, I enjoy sewing. Most of what I sew today involves either home decor, which often means long, straight seams without a whole lot of precision, or doll clothes that use hook and loop tape for closures rather than zippers or button holes!

So Dorcas was a model for me—as a seamstress. As I learned more about her, I also connected with her passion for helping those who needed her, the widows. In much of my professional life, I have been involved in helping people who live in poverty to have life-changing opportunities. I was particularly pleased when Dorcas herself joined me on the porch one day. She sat silently for at least half an hour while she stitched and slowly rocked. I had the sense that she was deliberately and intentionally connecting with my mood and energy level without saying a word. Finally, she whispered, "My child."

"Hello, Dorcas. How shall I follow in your footsteps? What are you calling me to do?"

She responded, "Oh, special child, I just did what needed to be done. I noticed these poor women as I walked the streets of Joppa. I knew that widows who had no male protector in their lives—a father, husband, or son—had no one to care for them. I began talking with them and discovered that they were absolutely delightful people. I knew their lives were not really very different from mine. Circumstances had placed them in a precarious situation, often through no fault of their own. I have to admit that a couple of the women were shrews, and I was not surprised that they had ended up as they had. But no matter. They still were needy. I decided that what these women desired was someone who would listen to them and find ways to help them with their basic necessities.

"I did not have many resources that could be used to house or feed them. However, I did know how to sew, and I had access to fine cloth. I discussed with the women what kinds of clothing they would like. I wanted them to have items that they felt beautiful wearing and that fit them well, both in size and personality. You know some people just say, 'Well, a widow should be grateful for anything I give her,' and then they give her some ugly, old, worn garment that no one would want to wear. I believed the women should have new garments, the same kinds of things I would put on. I certainly would not feel valued if I were wearing somebody's old rags!

"I began sewing. As the women realized what I was doing, they wanted to get involved. They cut or stitched alongside me. Some of them became my willing students, learning a skill that could help them with domestic duties if they were blessed to marry again or be welcomed into another family member's home. A few wanted to learn so they could earn a little money to help them with food or shelter. We all made wonderful garments. We laughed and talked and shared our lives as we stitched. Once we even had a fashion show, modeling the beautiful tunics and cloaks we had made.

"When I died the first time, my friends truly mourned me. What a blessing to me to realize that these women, to whom I thought I was reaching out from my benevolence, had claimed me as their friend and confidante. What they gave me in love and friendship more than repaid whatever I had given to them.

"My friend, look around you. See who is hurting. Look for those invisible folks in your community. There are lots of reasons that people get thrown away by their neighbors. Look for those people.

"When I got to know the widows, I earned their trust. I listened to them intently. I found out from them what would improve their lives. I did not assume that I knew what was best for them. I realized that their experience was not mine, and that I might not understand what was truly important to them.

"And then—this is important, so pay attention—I helped them learn the attitudes, skills, and confidence to do things for themselves that would improve their lives. I assisted when necessary but did not do things that they could and should do for themselves. For those widows who were unable to do the things necessary for a better quality of life, we all found ways to meet their basic human needs. Please do not ignore or abandon people who need extra care.

"Now all this may overwhelm you. Just remember we are all given different gifts. Use your God-given skills just as I used mine. You may work directly with widows because being with them may energize and excite you. On the other hand, if extended listening to them drains you, you might be gifted in organizing other people to help the widows. Maybe you can find the cloth they need for sewing or the money they require.

"Sometimes I wonder if my activities were what gave me a second chance at life. I don't know. I do know that my life was expanded and enriched beyond my wildest imaginings when Peter, under God's power, raised me from the dead. I suspect that when you give your life to others that you too will feel that you have received a second life.

"So … friend. Be a friend to people who often have no friends."

"I will, dear Dorcas. Thank you for being who you are." She rocked with me a while longer, and when she was satisfied that I was calm and full of peace, she left.

Dorcas' Call to Action

- My friend, look around you. See who is hurting. Look for those invisible folks in your community. There are lots of reasons that people get thrown away by their neighbors. Look for those people.

- Help people learn the attitudes, skills, and confidence to do the things for themselves that would improve their lives.

- Assist when necessary, but do not do things that others could and should do for themselves.

- Do not ignore or abandon people who need extra care.

- Use your God-given gifts just as I used mine.

- Be a friend to people who often have no friends.

Your Response to Dorcas' Presence

1. Do any of Dorcas' calls challenge you in your own life or community? If so, how?

2. Does her journey stir up a story for you? If so, what?

3. What did you learn from listening to Dorcas?

4. Does her story inspire you to action? If so, what? When? How? Why?

Porch Breezes

"Roshi Bernard Classman is a Zen teacher who runs a project for the homeless in Yonkers, NY. Last time I heard him speak, he said something that struck me: he said he doesn't really do this work to help others; he does it because he feels that moving into the areas of society that he had rejected is the same as working with the parts of himself that he had rejected."[42]

"Be not simply good; be good for something."[43]

"Start by doing what's necessary; then do what's possible; and suddenly you are doing the impossible."[44]

Chapter Thirty

Lydia—Networks of Support and Refusing to be Silenced

Acts 16:11–24

Lydia was a businesswoman, a seller of purple cloth, independent, and well-to-do. She was a God-fearer, attracted to the moral teachings of Judaism but not the ritual requirements. When Paul came to the place where she and the other women were praying in Philippi, Lydia heard the truth in his teachings. She and everyone in her household were baptized. As the first European convert, Lydia offered her home to Paul and the other missionaries.

For several years, I met every Friday morning with a couple of women friends for breakfast and deep conversation. We all have master of divinity degrees. Unlike me, though, one has an additional master's degree and the other earned a PhD. We each work in our professional lives to help others grow or change in positive, healthy ways. We all have grown children and are more or less the same age.

Our similarities are not why we come together, however. We need each other to help us walk paths that are uncharted by our mothers' generation. Our husbands, though supportive of our journeys, do not understand in their innermost beings the internal challenges and fears each of us face as we take what seem to us bold steps. When we struggle in dealing with employee issues, when we confront the powers that affect our lives, or when we think about significant career changes, we need each other's guidance, gentle yet confrontational questions, and compassionate acceptance of our fears and vulnerabilities.

We each have had others in our lives who thought they knew better than we did what we needed to do next in our careers. We have known in our hearts that our paths could only be discerned by our own inner wisdom. We have known how very difficult that task of discernment is. We know the challenges of taking steps to follow our most deeply held dreams and visions. We have known that we must see each other to sustain each of us as individuals.

Unfortunately, our respective schedules recently have meant that Friday mornings are no longer available to us. We feel fortunate when we are able to get together once or twice a year. When the externals of my life begin to affect my internal sense of equilibrium, I realize how much I need to be with my friends. When I know, just know, that something is trying to be born in me, I need the experience and comfort of their midwives' skills.

I was in such a place, feeling overwhelmed and out of control in the direction of my life. Because my friends could not be with me for another week or two, I went to the porch. I sat, wanting to cry, but no tears came. Then I felt someone standing behind me, massaging my shoulders to help me relax before she sat in the rocker. I looked at the woman's face and knew that she was here with some direction for me.

"Thank you for helping me begin to relax. What is your name?"

"I am Lydia."

I said, "Hello, Lydia. What are you calling me to do?"

She challenged and motivated me with her words. "Talk about a loaded question! There is so much I want to charge you with.

"I'll tell you first about being a businesswoman in a man's world. To run a business requires planning, diligence, political savvy, and sometimes even cunning. For a woman to have and use these skills was astounding to many of my contemporaries. I had to be wise and smart in multiple ways to compete with businessmen in the field. People thought my business would fail. Yet there I was, a *successful* woman in a business successful beyond imagination.

"Carry on my heritage of being a successful businesswoman. Pursue your goals even when others doubt or jeer at you. I worked hard, I loved my business, and I believed in myself. At times I was my only champion. Even my close advisors tried to 'advise' me off the path I knew I was to follow. Some of the men who worked for me tried to convince me that they should handle all the sales calls away from Thyatira, my home. Just think, if I had listened to them, I would not have been in Philippi and met Paul, and through him Jesus the Christ!

"I knew better than to listen without question to the caring advice of my employees. I knew that I was the best person to show the cloth, explain its quality, and broker our deals. I also knew that I could best work with the people who harvested the murex shellfish. Those folks could be an ornery lot because they knew their produce was the only way I could get my purple dyes. They knew they were essential to my business. I certainly did not want to trust my entire product line to someone who might anger my suppliers! So I stayed highly involved with every aspect of my business. I was the one with the drive and the vision. I had the most to lose if my business did not thrive.

"I pursued my business with intention and focus. I had people telling me that I could not do what was calling me. *I did not* believe them. I trusted my insights and judgment.

"I have to admit that my success was based on more than my business expertise. I also had a group of women who shared their lives with me just as I shared mine with them. They cheered me on. In some ways, I was their standard-bearer. They knew that I was doing what they could not or would not do. They did not ostracize me for how I chose to live my life. They were not jealous. Of course, at times, they asked me uncomfortable questions or raised their eyebrows, but they never closed their hearts to me.

"I valued their friendship and their comfort. I helped them in whatever ways I could. Because of my wealth, I was able to ease their financial situations sometimes. One or two of them sought my advice when they began small businesses of their own—baking sweets or weaving cloth.

"These women kept me sane and grounded. There is nothing like a group of sisters who nurture you and challenge you. When there is deep trust and abiding love among you, risks are easier to take.

"I hope you will gather such a circle around you.

"One of the things we did together was pray. Another in our group knew something about the God of Judah. She taught us what she had overheard when her husband brought his Jewish customers to their home. She was moved by the ways people were taught to honor others and to care for widows and orphans. Since we had a few widows in our group, we especially warmed to those concepts.

"We knew, though, that if the men heard us praying, they would have thought we were either crazy or radicals. So we went to the river, away from the traditional places of worship. There we could sing and pray, with first one and then another of us leading our worship and praise. That's where Paul found us.

"At first we stopped praying because we did not know who he was, why he was there, or what he would do to us. But he bid us to continue and even joined in.

"He taught us that the law, important as it was, was not the way to worship God. Then he told us about Jesus the Christ and the law of love.

"My heart fluttered, and my breathing quickened. I knew that this Jesus was a man who could expand my life rather than set limits on it, as other men had tried to do. I also knew that Jesus could teach me more about the Holy God. I wanted this power and this love and this commitment for myself and for every one of my employees and servants.

"From then on, Paul and any other missionaries of the Christ Way stayed in my home when they were in the area. I invited believers and seekers to my home to hear the gospel story from these travelers.

"As you explore your own path, discover ways you can support and nurture expansion of the faith, whether that is through befriending exhorters like Paul who teach the faith or by inviting people to partake of the glorious good news. Your life will be enriched as you open your heart to proclaiming the wondrous gospel of Jesus in whatever ways are appropriate for you and in whatever ways you can.

"And now, I must challenge you. Even though I was successful and independent, indeed a woman ahead of my time, and even though I had a group of wonderful female friends who loved me, and even though I helped spread the gospel, I was silenced by the church.

"The apostle Peter quoted the prophet Joel when he said, 'Your sons and your daughters shall prophesy.... Even upon my slaves, both men and women, in those days I will pour out my Spirit; and they shall prophesy' (Acts 2:17–18).

"But it did not happen. Well, actually it did happen, but our female voices were discounted and not valued. I was known and respected in the marketplace. My home was the worship center when Paul came to visit. Even so, I was well hidden and seen as only a servant in the religious establishment.

"My last charge to you, and the one that is most challenging, is do not be silenced. Use all your skills, talents, experiences, knowledge, hospitality, and support system to be heard. Your understanding of the faith is vital and important and worthy to be shared. Talk about it. Speak for me, for our sisters, for you, and most importantly, for our holy God."

"Lydia, what a mentor you are. Thank you for your guidance." She bustled off, as she had other things to do and other problems to solve.

Lydia's Call to Action

- Pursue your goals even when others doubt or jeer at you.

- Gather a circle of women around you who can keep you sane and grounded, who nurture you and challenge you, and with whom you share deep trust and abiding love.

- As you explore your own path, discover ways you can support and nurture expansion of the faith.

- My last charge to you, and the one that is most challenging, is do not be silenced. Use all your skills, talents, experiences, knowledge, hospitality, and support system to be heard. Your understanding of the faith is vital and important and worthy to be shared. Talk about it. Speak for me, for our sisters, for you, and most importantly, for our holy God.

Your Response to Lydia's Presence

1. Do any of Lydia's calls challenge you in your own life or community? If so, how?

2. Does her journey stir up a story for you? If so, what?

3. What did you learn from listening to Lydia?

4. Does her story inspire you to action? If so, what? When? How? Why?

Porch Breezes

"To put God's word into a human mouth was to push flesh to its limit.... It was like describing the Pleiades over a tin can telephone. And yet people did get it, because God commanded them. People still do it, although I am not sure we reckon it a risk anymore."[45]

"Mama exhorted her children at every opportunity to 'jump at de sun.' We might not land on the sun, but at least we would get off the ground."[46]

Afterword

After Lydia's visit, no more women from the Bible came to the porch. They had taught me what they wanted to share. They had embraced me with their wisdom. They had opened worlds of insight and challenge to me. They had given me gifts to share with others.

Many other people—flesh and blood people, both men and women—have come to the porch to talk, share a meal, cry, or laugh. It continues to be a holy place. I wish for you a porch of your own and friends to embrace you with calls to action. When you have sensed your call, I encourage you to follow it with all your heart, soul, mind, and strength.

About the Author

Beth Lindsay Templeton, director of Our Eyes Were Opened, a poverty education program, is a community activist, innovator, Presbyterian USA minister, consultant, teacher, and writer. She has been with United Ministries in Greenville, SC, for more than twenty-eight years and was executive director for twenty-four of those. She is the author of *Loving Our Neighbor: A Thoughtful Approach to Helping People in Poverty* and *Understanding Poverty in the Classroom*. She has interacted with people who are poor and marginalized, as well as with groups and individuals who want to help people who have minimal resources. She is a graduate of Presbyterian College and Erskine Theological Seminary. She and her husband have three married sons and four grandchildren.

Endnotes

1. "Facts About Hunger," accessed April 16, 2008, http://www.pcusa.org/hunger/learn.htm.

2. Annie E. Casey Foundation, http://www.aecf.org/MajorInitiatives/KIDS COUNT.aspx.

3. Plutarch, http://thinkexist.com/quotation/to_find_fault_is_easy_to_do_better_may-be/11772.html (accessed August 25, 2011).

4. Marva Dawn, *Joy in Divine Wisdom* (San Francisco: John Wiley and Sons, Inc., 2006), 23.

5. Mahatma Gandhi, *The Essential Gandhi*, ed. Louis Fischer (New York: Random House, 1962), 30.

6. W. H. Auden, "As I Walked Out One Evening," http://www.poemhunter.com/poem/as-I-walked-out-one-evening-3 (accessed August 15, 2011).

7. Beth Lindsay Templeton, "Psalm 130," sermon preached at McCarter Presbyterian Church, July 2000.

8. Story from United Ministries.

9. Robert Louis Stevenson, http://quotationspage.com/quote/27115.html (accessed August 15, 2011).

10. Martin Luther King, Jr., *Strength to Love* (Minneapolis: Fortress Press, 1981), 119.

11. "Statement of Belief," United Ministries, Greenville, SC.

12. Hugh F. Halverstadt, *Managing Church Conflict* (Louisville: Westminster John Knox Press, 1991), 28.

13. Eric H. F. Law, *Inclusion* (St. Louis: Chalice Press, 2000), 35.

14. David Lisak, "Rape Fact Sheet," http://www2.binghamton.edu/counseling/documents/RAPE_FACT_SHEET1.pdf (accessed September 4, 2008).

15. Beth Lindsay Templeton, "Prayer for February 10, 2011," Facebook entry.

16. Stephen L. Carter, *Integrity* (New York: Basic Books, 1996).

17. "Tamar's Voice: Ministering to Victims and Survivors of Clergy Sexual Abuse," http://www.tamarsvoice.org/home (accessed July 20, 2011).

18. Ingrid Bergman, http://thinkexist.com/quotation/you_must_train_your_intuition-you_must_trust_the/195048.html (accessed August 16, 2011).

19. Beth Lindsay Templeton, "A Prayer by Beth Lindsay Templeton," *United Ministries Newsletter*, October 2008.

20. Margaret Fuller, http://quotationsbook.com/quote/41869/ (accessed August 15, 2011).

21. Thomas Moore, http://www.manifestyourpotential.com/self_discovery/0_start_journey_self_discovery/being_unique/quotes_about_being_unique_inspirational.htm (accessed August 16, 2011).

22. Louisa May Alcott, http://thinkexist.com/quotation/i_am_not_afraid_of_storms_for_i_am_learning_how/213470.html (accessed August 16, 2011).

23. Marianne Williamson, *A Return to Love: Reflections on the Principles of "A Course in Miracles"* (New York: Harper Collins, 1992), 165.

24. Barbara Bush, http://abcnews.go.com/GMA/Books/story?id=124815&page=1 (accessed August 17, 2011).

25. Nicodemus, pseudonym of Melville S. Chaning-Pearce, *The Kingdom of the Real: An Existential Study of the First Phase of the Fourth Gospel* (London: Lutterworth Press, 1951).

26. Robert Louis Stevenson, http://www.quotationspage.com/quote/27115.html (accessed August 17, 2011).

27. Mahatma Gandhi, quoted in Louis Fischer, *The Life of Mahatma Gandhi* (New York: Harper, 1950), 102-103.

28. Beth Lindsay Templeton, Journal Entry, January 12, 2005.

29. Ann Weems, "Mary, Nazareth Girl," *Kneeling in Bethlehem* (Philadelphia: The Westminster Press, 1987), 25.

30. Anne Morrow Lindbergh, http://thinkexist.com/quotation/if_you_surrender_completely_to_the_moments_as/222513.html (accessed August 17, 2011).

31. Gail Godwin, *Evensong* (New York: Ballantine Books, 1999), 226.

32. "Listen to Me," http://lizditz.typepad.com/i_speak_of_dreams/2005/05/good_advice_but.html (accessed August 17, 2011).

33. Frances Moore Lappé and Anna Lappé, quoted from *Hope's Edge* in "Hope in Action," *Hope Magazine* (September/October 2003).

34. Terrence Fernsler, "Take Action for a Change: a Review of Jim Wallis' *Faith Works: Lessons from the Life of an Activist Preacher*," *Nonprofit World* 20 (July/August 2002).

35. Martin Luther King Jr. From a postcard purchased at the Martin Luther King, Jr. Center for Social Change.

36. "Hunger Facts and Materials," The Presbyterian Hunger Program, , http://gamc.pcusa.org/ministries/hunger/ hunger-facts-and-materials/ (accessed July 21, 2011).

37. National Low Income Housing Coalition, http://www.nlihc.org/oor/oor2011/ (accessed July 21, 2011).

38. Research supported by the Commonwealth Fund, *Health Affairs* (January/February 2008).

39. Martin Luther King, Jr., *Stride Toward Freedom: The Montgomery Story* (Boston: Beacon Press, 2010).

40. Ghanaian folk hymn.

41. Mother Teresa, http://web.stcecilia.wa.edu.au/uploads/newsletters/T2%20Wk%208%20-%2010%20June%202010.pdf (accessed on August 17, 2011).

42. Pema Chödrön, "When Things Fall Apart," *The Sun* 258 (June 1997).

43. Henry David Thoreau, http://thinkexist.com/quotation/be_not_simply_good-be_good_for_something/145681.html (accessed August 26, 2011).

44. St. Francis of Assisi, http://thinkexist.com/quotation/start_by_doing_what-s_necessary-then_do_what-s/219816.html (accessed August 17, 2011).

45. Barbara Brown Taylor, *When God is Silent* (Cambridge: Cowley Publications, 1998), 64.

46. Zora Neale Hurston, *Dust Tracks on a Road* (Philadelphia: J.B. Lippincott Company, 1942), http://www.quotationspage.com/quote/1832.html (accessed August 17, 2011).